THE ACTS
OF JOANNA

THE ACTS
OF JOANNA

Anne
Ortlund

THE ACTS OF JOANNA

ISBN 0-8499-0283-5
Library of Congress Catalog Card Number: 81-52523
Printed in the United States of America

*To the wonderful people of
Mariners Church, Newport Beach, who
have so graciously received our family
into their hearts and lives, this book
is respectfully dedicated.*

Contents

Contents

Prologue

Joanna: "Hello, there."

Anne: "Hello. Do I know you?"

Joanna: "I'm Joanna, the lead character in your first book of fiction."

Anne: "My what? I haven't written fiction since college days."

Joanna: "Think about it. I could be the perfect way to get your message across."

Anne: "I'm thinking. And I don't think so."

Joanna: "Why not?"

Anne: "I've got a lot of things on my heart to say that I think a story would hinder. How could I say them? They couldn't come out of *your* mouth."

Joanna: "Already you're insulting me, and you don't even know me?"

Anne: "I'm sorry. But—looking at you, you're just not the type."

Joanna: "You want to say them yourself?"

Anne: "I really do."

Joanna: "All right. I'm a very creative person. How about this? Tell my story, and now and then interrupt and say whatever you want to say."

Anne: "You're kidding. You mean, back and forth between fiction and nonfiction?"

Joanna: "Why not?"

Anne: "I've never heard of a book like that."

Joanna: "So? I think lurking inside of you is a person with wild, offbeat ideas."

Anne: "Already you're insulting me, and you don't even know me?"

Joanna: "That's cute. I just said that. I like you. I think we could work together."

Anne: "I don't know how the people of Word Books would take to it. Floyd Thatcher's opinion is important to me. He's very wise."

Joanna: "He'll love it."

Anne: "You're an aggressive person, aren't you?"

Joanna: "Of course. I'm a typical upper-class American female. I'm aggressive in expressing myself; I find great satisfaction in helping improve my community, in shaping cultural and educational efforts around me in Orange County, where I live.... Why shouldn't I make a place in one of your books? It will be new for you; it will be new for me."

Anne: "I'm aggressive, too, but I fight it."

Joanna: "I don't."

Anne: "Joanna, let your pretty green eyes look straight into mine. We're very different. There may be struggle ahead before our paths separate. Are you ready for whatever comes?"

Joanna: "Thank you for saying yes. I promise I'm ready."

*R*enewal Has a Beginning Time

1

The land curves gently into the Pacific Ocean at Corona del Mar, "Crown of the Sea," in Southern California. The "crown" is actually more like the softly rounded breasts of a woman in repose, whose blue-green dress of sea covers her not quite enough, though edged in ruffled foam lace. Around her wheel sea gulls, occasionally squealing their cry, and little private planes from the airport several miles inland.

Nature and man both like Corona del Mar. Indians enjoyed its perfect climate and its beauty perhaps fifteen thousand years ago. Into the nineteenth century Spain owned it, and then Mexico. In 1864 Jose Sepulveda sold this property and its surroundings to Flint, Bixby, Irvine, and Company for eighteen thousand dollars, an incredibly low price, even discounting inflation, when considering the billions of dollars of its present, scandalous worth. Just about a century ago, the first James Irvine became sole owner of the precious land. By that time, the larger area of coastland was already known as New Port, from whose docks cargoes of hides, tallow, livestock, and grain were shipped from the Irvine ranch.

The Acts of Joanna

Today Corona del Mar is the quiet, residential southern end of the City of Newport Beach. Inland from its beautiful public beach, smart specialty shops and famous gardens crowd together in coastal coziness.

Hugging the rounded bosom above are hundreds of terraced homes, recently built, their back sides snuggled against the hills, and their front sides, with deeply overhanging roof eaves, glassed to view the sea.

In the seaward patio of one such home sat Lady Magdalene, a cat. In quiet Sunday-morning sunshine she arched her back and stretched her body until every claw was fully extended. Eventually she gathered herself back, paused, and then stepped delicately along the terrazzo beside the pool.

Inside, upstairs, Joanna and her husband David were dressing for church. No words passed between them; Joanna was thinking what to wear.

She slipped into a favorite silk shirtwaist of periwinkle blue, and was surprised to slide the belt buckle to the last hole. I'm not eating, she thought.

Spectator pumps looked good to her, and her wonderful new soft leather bag. She checked the whole ensemble critically in her mirror—a gorgeous, floor-to-ceiling Baroque-framed mirror which dominated the bedroom and was her particular delight. In it she saw an angular woman with a deep tan, penetrating green eyes, and a wonderful mane of thick black hair, worn short and smooth for tennis. She was thankful for the "body" in her hair, which helped fill out the thin face with its precise nose and high cheekbones. Joanna was not beautiful, but she was striking and intelligent-looking, and she was glad she wore tailored clothes particularly well. She moved closer to the mirror and wondered why there seemed so many strain lines around her eyes. With one finger she smoothed a little extra makeup around them and reached for her dark glasses.

To the kitchen for a glass of orange juice. How messy her desk looked, nearby! Thought Joanna, the litter seemed to reflect the state of her life. Why was there never enough time? She needed to answer that stack of letters and mail fabric samples back to the decorator. There was that half-finished letter of complaint to their congressman. And she hadn't yet registered for the consumer-awareness course, or cancelled her golf lesson, or offered Betsy their house for bridge this week. And somehow she wanted to get out of that church committee. . . . Why had they asked her, anyway? She wasn't *that* involved in church. . . .

Suddenly she realized that David was standing in the kitchen and had finished his juice. A glance at the clock, and they were into the garage, into the brown Mercedes, and into the mid-morning sunshine, driving through half-deserted residential streets.

The church courtyard seemed a little fuller than usual. Though she and David had said little to this point, suddenly, surrounded by the Beautiful People, they burst into animation.

"Wow, Tony, check those trou-*sers!* You gotta be ready for eighteen holes this afternoon, right?"

"Mary Beth, you look wonderful! I haven't seen you in ages. You've lost weight; you look ter*rif*ic!"

"How sweet of you, George! Thanks for the coffee, but I forgot my sugar substitute. How 'bout putting in a teeny-weeny bit of sugar for me? Will it poison my whole system?"

Eventually the huggers and chatterers swirled slowly out of the patio—leaving behind table-piles of white plastic cups stained with coffee and lipstick—and into the inner recesses of the church. There the service was already in progress, and they hurriedly slipped into pews and caught up with the singing of the hymn by at least the final stanza.

Joanna and David joined the others in a little standing, a little sitting, a little unison reading and this and that, and a settling down for the sermon.

"Let me read for you today Ephesians 4:17-24 in *The Living Bible,*" the pastor began.

Joanna sat as still as the others, and mused over a rather creative (she thought) concept of the congregation: that they sat dappled in sunlight and shade—those in the sunlight listening with interest to what the minister was saying, and those in the shade not very involved. She and David were admittedly in a patch of shade.

"Let me say this, then, speaking for the Lord: Live no longer as the unsaved do, for they are blinded and confused. Their closed hearts are full of darkness; they are far away from the life of God because they have shut their minds against him, and they cannot understand his ways. . . ."

Now, that doesn't sound very positive, thought Joanna. What an advertising approach, if indeed the pastor is trying to sell his subject. . . .

"But that isn't the way Christ taught you! If you have really heard his voice and learned from him the truths concerning himself, then throw off your old evil nature—the old you that was a partner in your evil ways—rotten through and through, full of lust and sham. . . ."

Joanna blocked out the words. How brown my hand is, next to David's, she mused.

"Now your attitudes and thoughts must all be constantly changing for the better. Yes, you must be a new and different person, holy and good. Clothe yourself with this new nature. . . ."

Joanna looked at the women around her, and it seemed as if a disproportionate number wore polyester and obviously did their own hair. She recrossed her stockinged legs, wondered how much she was wrinkling the back of her silk dress as she sat on it, admired her spectators again, and was glad she had slipped on her sapphire ring. Its blue did not match the periwinkle blue of her dress; she felt good that she knew how to mix-match with casualness.

"I want to teach a principle today," the paster was continuing, "the principle of renewal—of constant newness with God. This should be the constant, never-deviating state of our church, and this should be the constant, never-deviating state of our own personal lives. Romans 6:4 says that just as God resurrected Christ his Son to eternal newness, so he wants you and me to live in constant 'newness of life.'

"Let me quote a book I was reading this week:

"Life is shaped like a funnel. But everything depends on which way you go into it.

"The worldling goes in at the big end, where everything looks grandiose and inviting and limitless in possibilities and freedom. Then life for him narrows down into boring smallness.

"The Christian goes in at the other end; "narrow is the gate" that leads to his life. But then he finds that it broadens out into beautiful freedom, into glorious newness. It keeps opening and opening and opening into God's vast will and righteousness and pleasures. There is no boredom! There is no smallness when you walk with God.

"Within that life in him there is continual newness and expansion. You can begin again and again and again!"[1]

Briefly Joanna thought about this. A funnel. Well, she hadn't noticed life broadening lately. Was it narrowing? One thing was certain—it was piling higher with picky details of things to do.

"See first with me *The Promise of God For a New Beginning.* . . ."

The minister's message faded in and out of Joanna's mind. She heard bits and pieces: "be renewed in the spirit of your mind . . . live in fresh newness of life. . ."

"Renewal is actually both a crisis and a process," he was saying. "Once the crisis has happened, the growing Christian *normally experiences* constant renewal. If your Christian life is healthy and normal, you *will be* in continual renewal—continual revival.

"How are you doing spiritually, compared with six months ago? Are you experiencing God's renewing?"

Joanna studied the people in front of her, wondering if anyone she knew felt all that renewed from six months before. Her eyes rested on Clare and Roger Hartford. Well, probably they felt that way. Clare and Roger were the most religious couple Joanna knew. She had always been a little awed and intimidated by them; they seemed so *together.*

If they'd been dowdy, she'd have been more comfortable with them, actually. But there was Roger with his medium brown hair waving gently behind his ears, and his dark brown suit coat fitting his shoulders perfectly. And Clare looked lovely in a turquoise knit; and Joanna studied approvingly the design of the gold earring, studded with one small, flashing diamond, in Clare's delicate, pierced ear.

But obviously, all their attention was not on anything except the pastor's words, and that's what made them so *together.*

"Let's look at *the plans of God for a new beginning.* Oh, when your personal life is caught up into *his* plans, you've moved into his strategies for the whole universe! God is on his way to making 'all things new,' says Revelation 21:5. He knows about the smog. He says through the psalmist that the earth and the heavens 'will perish . . . they will all wear out like a garment. Like clothing [God] will change them, and they will be discarded.'[2]

"And in Isaiah 65:17–18 God says, 'Behold, I will create new heavens and a new earth. The former things will not be remembered, nor will they come to mind. But be glad and rejoice forever in what I will create!' The whole plan of God ends in renewal, in newness!"

Joanna had picked up the word *smog.* With so little smog here along the coast, she thought, I'll bet our property values will just keep rising and rising.

"And, friends, you should experience this newness, this re-creation, in your Christian life as well. In your affections, in your mind, this world's things should grow old to you, and become unworthy, uninteresting, outdated, used up. While the things of

God should become more and more real to you, more and more valuable, more and more splendid—by miracle, constantly new!

"The angel announced Jesus' birth saying, 'I bring you good news of great joy.' Did you ever realize that God's news is the only news that's continually *news?* Today's news will be old tomorrow. But the gospel is always 'new news.' That's miracle.

"And this is God's eternal principle. So when we stay close to him, our whole earthly life is continually fresh; we are constantly breaking into newness. Says Proverbs 4:18, 'The path of the righteous is like the first gleam of dawn, shining ever brighter until the full light of day.'

"What if we get stuck in oldness, in sameness? Then we need to recognize that we've gotten away from the Lord, and repent of that. And he is always ready to bring us back to newness."

Suddenly Joanna thought, there are parts of this service that are rather interesting. I wish our minister preached shorter sermons, and they used more time for music and things like testimonies by lay people. What he's saying is right, I'm sure, but it's just so *dull.* She thought her back was beginning to ache a little, and she wondered if she should write a letter to the church and tell them if they wanted to keep growing, they'd be smart to invest in seat cushions.

"But see with me *the price of a new beginning,*" continued the voice up front.

Joanna had had enough. She switched off her mind. I'll buy the tape of it and maybe hear it later, she thought. That'll give the church a little business, too. . . .

Joanna and David were soon home again. The house seemed wonderfully cool and dark. Joanna wriggled out of the periwinkle silk, and out of her girdle, and put them away. In her shorts and bare feet she pulled some steaks from the freezer, and realized that she'd forgotten to feed Lady Magdalene this morning.

Suddenly she wondered if she had a dull headache coming on.

2

The Sunday afternoon sun was sinking beyond the craggy outline of Catalina Island in the distance and into the golden sea. A chill crept into the air, and Joanna gathered up the bulky Sunday papers strewn around the pool and went indoors. David was in the den—pacing, she thought, and she looked at him.

"Joanna," he said, and cleared his throat as he seldom did unless a speech was coming on; Joanna had a flash of thought that this might be the first interesting moment of the entire Sunday so far. "I've been waiting for you to come in. In fact, I've been waiting all day. I've gotta try to tell you something."

There he stood, his big frame just slightly overfilling his beautiful shirt and pants, and confusion making red blotches on his handsome, sandy-complected face. Suddenly she saw that that familiar face of his was already aging a little—maybe from tension, or from his tendency to overdrink, or both.

"I'm trying to think how to say this, Joanna. Cripes, I don't think I'm gonna come up with the right words, no matter how I say it. . . ." He jingled the keys in his pocket, and his eyes didn't often meet hers.

"The fact is, the way things are with you and me, I'm just bored to hell. I've tried to hint to you that maybe we ought to see a shrink or something—maybe go see the pastor, I don't know—but you don't hear me; I can't get through; you're off in space somewhere; you're out to lunch. And I used to care. By God, I cared for a long time. I cared for years. But I don't care any more."

"David," queried Joanna, "are you drunk? What are you saying? I don't believe you! I don't *believe* you!"

He was beginning to cry!

"Joanna," he went right on, "you're sharp, you're pretty, you're terrific, I guess, and that's why I fell for you, but we've got nothing between us any more. We've got *nothing.*"

Joanna was aware that her body was trembling dreadfully inside, and she clenched her fists for control.

His voice was rising. "You won't believe it, but I've been faithful to you to this very moment, and I'm frustrated to hell. I've tried to be a good boy; I've tried to go it the church's way, and stay nice for all your churchy friends. . . ."

Like a junior higher making his first speech, he was rocking back and forth and awkwardly throwing his arms around, punching out the sentences between sobs.

"I'm going somewhere. I'm gonna get me a woman who'll turn me on—"

"David!" raged Joanna. "What kind of television have you been watching? We've been having a perfectly decent Sunday, and suddenly out of the blue you hit me with all this—this *garbage!* What have I done to you to bring this on? What have I done? What on earth is the matter with you?"

"Hah! You're listening," he cried. "Finally I got your attention. This is the first meaningful conversation we've had for months. The first, and maybe the last. . . . Oh, Joanna!"—and in a gush of agony he fell across the room and put his arms around her—"Where are you? I've lost you! I can't find you any more!"

Joanna shut her eyes, feeling the tears squeeze out, and kept her trembling body rigid. How could she surrender to someone who had just stabbed her in the stomach? She was furious. Surely he would apologize; surely now he'd take back what he said. . . .

Gradually David's sobs lessened. His arms relaxed. He fished for a handkerchief and blew his nose. He looked terrible, all blotched and wet, even in his reddish hair, and he looked at her with swollen eyes.

"Joanna," he said calmly at last, "let's try a separation for a little while. Don't worry; I won't be far. I'll find a motel. I can come write the checks twice a month, and if there's anything a repair man can't handle, let me know."

Joanna sank down into a chair. "This isn't real." she said. "You're bluffing."

She saw him go through the door to the garage and come back with a suitcase.

She heard him tramp around for a while upstairs.

She turned her back. "This isn't real," she repeated to herself, out loud.

She heard him go clumsily through the door to the garage again, and heard the electric garage door go up.

She heard his little sports Fiat start up, and back out.

By the time the garage door had gone down again, she could no longer hear the purr of the little Fiat driving away.

Then she screamed. And she burst into weeping that lasted up the stairs, and as she fell onto her bed, and for a long time afterward.

Later Joanna wandered restlessly about the house, not knowing what to do, whom to tell. Her parents were dead. She certainly wouldn't tell Stevie and Missie, away in college—heavens, no! She tried to think of her friends, her church friends. The realization came to her that she had no really close friends, only social buddies who would be shocked and spread the news—as she herself had often done when it had happened to others.

"It." Joanna didn't know what else to call this thing except "it." Surely it wasn't really a split. She and David had had twenty-four years together, and there was too much to lose, just like *that*. She realized she had loved that man a long time. And upset or not, he was hers.

Surely he had just been in a bad mood and would show up at bedtime. Otherwise, where would he go? This was ridiculous.

David would be back and apologize by bedtime.

3

It was the next morning when Joanna crept to the telephone on the nightstand beside her bed. Did her little book have Clare Hartford's number in it? Clare would know what to tell her to do.

Clare's number was there, and Joanna dialed it. Some stupid cleaning woman answered the phone, and Joanna thought if she had to wait for Clare too long, she'd be trembling too hard to talk. Finally—

"Hello-o!" trilled a singsong voice in two tones like a door chime.

"Oh, God," gritted Joanna through her teeth, and she decided she'd phoned a stupid Pollyanna who lived her stupid, grinning life in stupid unreality. . . . She hung up.

She sat there for a long while. Then she remembered the taped sermon she'd brought home yesterday. She fished it out of her purse and put it in the bedroom stereo's tape deck.

She listened from the beginning. "O God, I'm your child," she whispered. "I don't know much, but I'm your child. What are you saying to me? How can I get David back? I've got to pay attention to this tape, to whatever you can say to me."

She listened again to the pastor's first point—"The promises of God for a new beginning." It didn't seem as dull as it had yesterday.

"The plans of God for a new beginning."

Why does he have to start all his points with *p*?, she fretted to herself. Why do preachers have to talk in such stuffy words? Why can't he just *talk*? But she needed what he was saying, so she settled down to listen.

"The price of a new beginning," he announced on the tape, and she hardly noticed irritation over another *p* because this was where she'd switched him off.

"There is a cost for renewal."

Don't give me rough stuff, winced Joanna. I've just had a terrible night, and all I want is some comfort. . . . But she tried to listen.

"It does cost," the tape went on relentlessly. "It takes courage to repent, to change. Why does renewal seem so difficult? *Your greatest opposition to renewal is you.* There is in all of us an internal resistance, a downward drag. You have inside of you a longing to be fresh and new, but you also have, inside your old nature, that strange reluctance which resists change, and which whispers lies to you that the new way might be no fun. . . .

"Jesus shook his head over Jerusalem and wept, saying, 'O Jerusalem, Jerusalem, . . . how often I have wanted to gather your children together, as a hen gathers her chicks under her wings, but you were not willing.'

"But listen, my Christian friends: you can expect that, in this tug-of-war between you and your Savior, *He will win.* God loves you too much to let you get by with the status quo. If you're rebellious, or if you're even just indifferent, *only a careless God would ignore it.*"

Joanna felt uncomfortable and fidgety. Maybe she should contact Betsy about that bridge date. . . .

"God has great purposes for the whole universe—and he has great purposes for *you.*

"He is in the fabulous business of '*bringing sons to glory*'!—and *you can expect renewal or judgment.* If you are not prepared for personal renewal, God will judge you—not in penal judgment, as he will unbelievers, but in corrective judgment. He will make life miserable for you!

"That's why he pleads with you in Acts 3:19: 'Repent, then, and turn to God, so that your sins may be wiped out, that times of refreshing [renewal] may come from the Lord'!"

The words were continuing tenderly—something about being "transformed by the renewing of your mind"—but Joanna ejected the tape. It was hard to concentrate. Her mind kept switching back to David—or even to little irritations like the decorator's need for those fabric samples. God! Life was *stupid.*

She sat on her big bed and ran her fingers through her mane of black hair. At that moment she could think of no alternative to calling Clare back again. She dialed the number. This time that irritating singsong came on directly:

"Hello-o!" In exactly the same pitches.

"Clare?" Joanna spoke with effort. "This is Joanna Heston. Could I see you? I'm sorry to bother you; maybe you're too busy. . . . I just thought I'd ask. . . ." Her throat seemed too congested for her voice to push out anything else.

"Joanna, my dear, something's the matter. What can I do? What is it?"

"Well—David and I had a fight, and he's walked out, and . . . I don't know what to do." She was crying weakly.

"Joanna, where are you? Are you home?"

"Yes," said Joanna.

"I'll come over right now. Where do you live, again? I was there once for a reception, remember?—but it's been a while. Refresh my memory."

Joanna gave her directions and hung up. She looked at herself in her wonderful Baroque-framed mirror—what a magnificent mirror!—and decided she didn't look too rumpled to receive Clare. She had put on an orange tee shirt and beige wrap-around cotton skirt and her leather-thonged barefoot sandals this morning. She had on no makeup, but she said out loud, "Okay, so I look like a woman scorned."

The words made her stomach convulse a little.

"I'm acting in a play" came through her teeth. "This isn't really happening."

She made her way down the stairs, sliding her hand along the darkly polished banister. The house seemed serene as a funeral parlor. Everything was in place to receive a visitor. Should they sit in the living room? It seemed too stiff. On the patio? Any little breeze might make her shake again.

In the den, she decided. Should she make some tea? She started into the kitchen and began to wish Clare weren't coming—and then the door chimes announced that she had.

The two of them found their way to the den, and they dropped down into the big couch together.

"I came in my grubby jeans," apologized Clare. "And I was putting out begonias, and I didn't even have time to get the dirt out of my fingernails. Every time I don't bother with gloves, I get caught."

Her hand touched Joanna's knee, and she turned serious. "Tell me whatever you want to say, Joanna."

For a long time Joanna's heart poured out. Occasionally, dimly, she heard the grandfather clock's mellow baritone, but mostly she was occupied with David and herself. She recounted the security of her life: that David's long hours of work, his regularity, and his predictability made her life easy; that she was free to pursue her own interests, especially now that Stevie and Missie were away in college. She and David argued a lot, but didn't all married couples? Anyway, they weren't alone together all that much, because they usually did their socializing with other couples.

Somehow, the rush of words propelled Joanna into another subject, almost without her willing it. She and David knew there were people around like Clare and her family, who took their Christianity terribly seriously, but none of their closer friends were like that. Nevertheless, since as a child she'd accepted Christ, she'd occasionally wondered how much she was missing, and wished she knew the Bible better, but she and David were so busy. . . .

It was embarrassing, but she was weeping. Arms went around her. From somewhere a Bible appeared. Words were said, but Joanna heard none of them. Actually, now that her story was out, she began to feel a little relieved, and was starting to think that maybe she could handle this new situation by herself.

Eventually she saw Clare to the door, and was glad she hadn't committed herself to anything further.

4

It was later that afternoon, when Joanna backed the Mercedes out of the sunlit driveway to get some groceries, that she saw a basket of begonias at her front door. She stepped out of the car to look, and tucked in between the bright green leaves was scribbling on Clare Hartford's notepaper:

Dear Joanna,
Thanks for giving me the privilege of sharing a little piece of your life this morning. I thought you might like to know that each Tuesday evening from seven thirty to nine thirty a little discipling group of couples and singles meets in our home with Roger and me. I think you'd probably know them from church.
We'd love to have you join us if you'd like to.

Joanna stuck the basket inside the door and backed out of the driveway. A silly old song was in her mind: "She didn't say yes, she didn't say no. . . ."
Nevertheless, when the grandfather clock chimed seven the next

evening. she was toying with the idea and wondering what she would wear. Pants, she thought, would be casual for an intimate group. She slipped into a rust-colored silk shirt and creamy white wool pants, and clasped some heavy gold chains around her neck. For class, she said to herself, as she looked in the full-length Baroque mirror. Joanna, you do have class. She threw over her shoulder a bulky-knit grey-beige sweater.

As Joanna turned away, her stomach wrenched suddenly, and her heart cried, David, where are you? What are you doing now? Predictable David; in the daytime she could picture him. But this evening?

The thoughts were too painful. She gathered up her things and went downstairs and out to the car.

The Hartfords' address was easy to find; the street was a well-known one in Corona del Mar's residential area. Joanna found as she looked for the number that she had driven around to the backside of Corona's lovely hills.

"No ocean view," she sniffed. knowing that automatically took fifty thousand dollars off the value of the house. Still, when she found the address, she was impressed. The home was a country-French purist's dream, with steeply sloping roof lines, shuttered windows with small panes, and in the flower beds tightly packed marigolds that almost shouted their enthusiasm. She loved the brick entryway; she loved the cozy warmth inside; she loved the plain cream walls, the dark wood floors, and the floral chintzes of red and bottle green. Obviously professionally decorated, she assessed, and skillfully reflecting the owners' warmth and charm.

She followed Clare into the family room, counter-separated from the kitchen, and bright with pieces of brass. Quality brass, noted Joanna, and nice antiques. Could they have inherited things? Or was Roger's job more important than she had realized? She wondered what he did, but there was no more time to assess and wonder. Her face froze into a smile of civility as she was introduced.

She was surprised that she knew everybody in the group, at least by sight. Besides Roger and Clare there were one other couple and three singles—a man and two women. Probably all divorced, she thought. And now I'm one more woman, adding to the imbalance.

Still, they seemed to welcome her warmly as they stood around with plates of fruit, cheeses, and coffee cups.

"This is de-caf coffee," explained Fred the bachelor, as he poured her some. "There's no poison in this kind."

One of the girls piped up, "I hear there's poison in de-caf, too."

"Joanna, where's David tonight?" asked Susie, the other wife.

"Oh, he's got business tonight." Joanna stone-walled. "He's sorry he couldn't come along." Then she caught Roger's eye. He probably knows, she thought!

"Hey, forget the fruit and cheese," cried one of the girls. "Clare's bringing out the good stuff!"

Clare had appeared with a platter of finger tarts. "Well, you're all counting calories," said Clare, "but then I felt guilty offering you *just* fruit—"

"Put the fruit in the refrigerator!" crowed Fred. "Yum, yum!"

Eventually Roger broke through the banter and pulled them all into the living room. "Folks, this is going to be worth wading into tonight," he said, "so let's get going."

"We're starting a new study tonight on ACTS—not the book in the Bible, but A-C-T-S, which is an old formula for a meaningful prayer time: A for adoration; C for confession; T for thanksgiving; and S for supplication.

"But I'm in a weekly small group with Pastor John, as you know; and he's been thinking lately about how ACTS is really a formula for *all* our Christian living, not just for prayer. He's been leading us in a study of it."

Joanna stared at him, fascinated. She had never noticed before that when Roger put his lips together for sounds like *b* and *m* and *p*, he pursed them a little and made a dimple come at the corner of his mouth. He's darling, she thought. How does anyone concentrate on what he's saying when he looks so cute?

It was something about the preacher's group of guys praying with him over his sermons. . . .

"He's really burdened about our church's getting off the dime and getting really renewed in the Lord. How about that sermon last Sunday? Right in there, boy. And you notice the way he's really leaning into his messages lately has started swelling the size of the crowd. Something's gonna happen in our church. Wow, let it come. . . . Joanna, can we get you a Bible?"

Bible: two *b*s, two dimples. He's darling. Oh, he's talking to me—!

"Uh—oh, no, as a matter of fact, I don't have one with me. . . ." Clare put up her finger and disappeared.

"Anyway, the A-C-T-S study in our group has been so rich, I asked Pastor John if I could turn around and pass it on to you. And after a while he's gonna preach on it, so this'll get us ready. We'll be in on the ground floor."

One more pot of de-caf made the rounds, and Clare handed the extra Bible to Joanna, who promised to bring her own next time, and they settled in.

Only one moment marred the evening. That was when "adoration" of God led to a discussion of affirmations in the marriage relationship, and Susie said,

"I can always tell a good, stable marriage when I see one. Like Joanna and David. They look so cute together, and they're obviously rock-solid, whole, steady people. I've never known them well, but I've always admired them so much.

"Joanna, I'll bet you and David really affirm each other a lot, right?"

And Joanna piped up brightly. "Oh, right, right!"

And kept her eyes off Clare.

A Stands for Adoration

5

Anne: "Joanna, it's time for me to butt in."
Joanna: "Please do."
Anne: "You don't mind?"
Joanna: "I'm uptight from recent events, and I could use a rest."
Anne: "All right, thanks. Fade off the scene, please, dear. I need to talk about you...."

Poor Joanna! I know her plight well. Even as a Christian, she's flailing around, trying to make her life come together through her own human efforts.

Joanna and her friends are the products of my imagination, although she and David are typical of hundreds of couples around Ray and me here in Corona del Mar, where we live. But Ray is not—repeat, not—the pastor in this story, nor is our Mariners Church, or any church around, Joanna's and David's church.

I'll get back to their story soon, but briefly let's look at what it is Pastor John is studying, and what Roger is passing on to his group.

Adoration, confession, thanksgiving, and supplication.

Here are four concepts almost foreign to Joanna. Maybe to you, too? I don't know where you are in your spiritual pilgrimage, but there are thousands like Joanna and David, who attend church more often than not and would fervently maintain they're Christians, *but.* . . .

They know facts *about* God, but they don't know God. A mental attitude of continually worshiping and "adoring" him probably doesn't even seem appealing. It smacks of fanaticism.

They certainly aren't into "confession," even if they've tried the small-group thing. Share your weakness to somebody, and—who knows—later on it could keep you from a job promotion.

"Thanksgiving"? For all they know, it's simply a day to stuff yourself on a turkey dinner and then watch football.

And supplication—well, maybe they could buy that one. It's probably an old-fashioned word that's supposed to represent asking God for things. Only nowadays they and their friends are more into meditation, affirmation, or goal visualization.

Joanna's going to get confronted with these four concepts as four steps to strengthening the most important life priority, her relationship with God.[3]

And they can be four succeeding steps to your own personal spiritual renewal as well—the renewal Pastor John was preaching on, not only to his own congregation, but also to you and me. I'm excited to write about these for myself, too, and I'm praying, "Lord, teach me as I write! Work these four ingredients deeply into my life and into the readers', too."

First, think about your adoration of God, your preoccupation with him as the mental framework for all of your living. As Robert Cook says, "Christianity is not a point of view, it's a love affair with a Person!" I might add, it's not even any *fun* unless it's a love affair with a Person—Jesus Christ.

The other day a friend was commenting to me how much Ray and I are alike. She said, "You think so much like him. Theologically, your mind works like his; you're excited about the same truths. You even look alike!" Nothing she could have told me is more complimentary to me!

Well, if we're somewhat alike, part of the reason must be that we have spent a lot of time together for the last thirty-five years. And for the last maybe fifteen years, we've spent our Tuesdays studying together—which means we've discovered truths together and grown and learned together.

But I think the main reason I may be growing like him (if I am) is just that I admire him so much. When you think a lot about somebody, and look at him or her a lot, you tend to copy that person—whether you realize it or not.

So it is with us and the Lord. The more we're occupied with him, admiring and "adoring" him, the more we'll be like him. And the more we'll be lifted into his beauty and truth and goodness. "Adoration" will become the happiest way of life we've ever known.

Actually, once we get our eyes focused on him, the scene around us is Dullsville! Look into the eyes of a person who talks endlessly about money or fashions or sports or TV shows or cars or food. The eyes are beginnnng to dim with monotony and disappointment and stress. Aren't they? Do you see it? Look in the mirror. How about your own?

Adoration of God puts us in a new ballpark. It's holy. It's wonderful. Adoration is looking into the face of God, into that bright, pure light, and loving just *looking* in admiring wonder.

When we pray, let's start with adoration. *He'll* love it. We'll love it.

All of us spend a lot of time in earthly pursuits. But sometimes does your heart hunger for something more? And do you wonder what you're missing? This little life of yours is just a piece of eternity. What are they doing on the other side? They're worshiping God! They're on their faces before him. Revelation 4 and 5 tell about it. In concentric circles, far out to limitless horizons, everyone is gathered around him! Cecil B. de Mille never thought up a scene so grand.

We're just short-sighted, dull little ants busying around a golf-ball planet. but the Larger Scene, the eternal one, is full of the adoration of God.

When Jesus told us to pray, "Thy will be done *on earth as it is in heaven*"—that's what's happening in heaven: worship! Then worship is obviously, first and foremost, his will.

But be warned, before you read the next chapter. Worshiping God is radical. It's a change in posture—for life. You may look upright on the outside, but in your mind you'll be flat on your face before him. You'll be continually awed and overwhelmed by him.

We could mention a lot of positive results, but nevertheless—

One split-second glimpse of who he really is—and you'll feel smashed, ruined, undone, embarrassed, broken.

6

Once General Omar Bradley (so the story goes) was flying commercially and wearing civilian clothes. He hoped nobody would sit in the plane seat next to him, because he had a lot of paperwork to do. But sure enough, someone sat down.

And not just anyone, but a very over-friendly, gum-chewing young Army private in uniform. Not having any idea who the General was, the young rookie said,

"Hey, fella, if we're gonna fly together for two hours, we better get acquainted, right?"

He stuck out his hand. "I'm Harry."

"How do you do," said General Bradley.

"Lemme see, I'm gonna guess what you do. You look like a top salesman to me," the kid said.

"No," said General Bradley.

"No? Ya mean this terrific brain of mine missed it? Then I bet you're a big businessman."

"No," said General Bradley. "I'm in the same outfit you are, son. I'm in the Army."

"You gotta be a sergeant, then. Top sergeant?"

The General had had enough. "Young man, I am Omar Bradley, five star general, and Chief of Staff of the Joint Chiefs of Staff of the armed forces of the United States of America."

"Izzat right, General?" The kid popped his gum. "You've got a big job. Don't mess it up!"

Yes, generals, presidents, governors, school teachers, cops, parents—authorities of all kinds today "don't get no respect." And who can measure the resulting confusion, inefficiency, nervous tension, and worse?

What can happen to a school whose principals and teachers are belittled or ignored? What can happen to a war when generals are belittled or ignored? Any system whose head is neglected can go out of control and into panic or decay.

Think about your own life, up to this very moment. If you've been like Joanna and David, Christians underrating their Head—can you imagine the resulting lack of direction, wear and tear, inefficiency, confusion, fatigue, and downright suffering?

Come with me. Let me lead you gently (and Christ lead both of us) to what "adoration" is all about—a mindset, a lifestyle of worship.

The word *worship* in the Bible literally means "to bow." The idea is to make ourselves lower, to say that God is higher. As the word *shaha* in the Hebrew, it appears one hundred times in the Old Testament. In the New Testament it's the Greek word *proskeneo*, and is used fifty-nine times. It's the way people defer to God, or even to each other.

In the Bible God's good people bowed a lot.

Do you remember the story of Joseph's being sold into Egypt as a slave by his jealous brothers? Many years later, when they were starving, and came crawling and bowing to the Prime Minister of Egypt to get food—they discovered they were bowing to their long-lost brother. *Shaha* is the word used.

Or remember when young David, rising in power, sent and asked beautiful Abigail to be his wife? And she bowed with her face to the ground and said, "Oh, yes, yes, yes!" (or something like that)? *Shaha* is the word used—even though when she went to join him, she brought along five of her own maids. She wasn't bowing to say, "I'm nobody"; she was just bowing to say, "You're wonderful." That's *shaha*.

In Western culture we don't bow to people. Too bad. But how we need to learn the spirit behind the bowing! It implies graciousness, deference—an attitude of serving, helping, lifting.

On the other hand, one of the characteristics of the evil "last days" before Christ's return to earth is that people *will not "bow,"* that is, they will refuse to recognize that anyone is higher than themselves. "Bold and arrogant," the Bible calls them, and says they will "reject authority. [They will] speak abusively against whatever they do not understand." That's the gum-popping private!

In the Bible God has a vivid picture of people whose life-attitude is unbowing: he calls them "stiff-necked." Isn't that descriptive? They're upright, looking you straight in the eye, utterly unaware of any personal inadequacy. They have no humility.

And their lack of humility toward each other is just a symptom of a deeper problem: lack of humility toward God. Think how most of them saunter, heads up, in and out of churches every Sunday. Their "body language" gives them dead away. I'm not speaking of liturgy, but of life-attitude—which shows! Tozer speaks of "self-confident, bustling worshipers"[4]—really a contradiction of terms.

But what if we truly get a view of God? Holy Toledo! He's not a funny, shuffling little old man in the movies.

He is tenderness and mercy. He is holiness—blinding white. He is the loftiness of power, laughing derisively at rebellious nations and biding his time. He is the hot, sudden violence of wrath. The slow, tumbling aeons of ages are in his scope. He is intimacy and fun with his loved ones. He is the blazing jealousy, the sweet, groaning pain, the tender wonder of lover's love.

Ezekiel caught a glimpse—and fell face downward.

John did, too—and fell down as though dead.

So did Isaiah—and he cried, "I'm ruined!" But in a moment God cleansed him, and then he wanted to serve him forever.

Yes, if we come to understand anything about God, our sins become enormous to us! King David cried,

> My guilt has overwhelmed me
> like a burden too heavy to bear. . . .
> I am bowed down and brought very low;
> all day long I go about mourning (Ps. 38:4, 6).

And Ezra! He identified himself so with all the wicked people around him that he fell to his knees and prayed,

> O my God, I am too ashamed and disgraced to lift up my face to you, my God, because our sins are higher than our heads and our guilt has reached to the heavens (Ezra 9:6).

I can think of two reasons why we might always walk around casually before God, with our heads held high: if we never sinned at all, or if we were gods equal with him. Since neither of these is true, maybe we'd better take another look at Moses. When God appeared to him in the burning bush, he "hid his face, because he was afraid to look at God" (Exod. 3:6).

Oh, it really is true that God invites us to "approach the throne of grace with confidence."

But first we have to know that it's a throne of *grace*. We're not just to kick open the barroom door and bust in. When we see who we are, and who he is, we ought to get so trembling and weak-kneed that he has to urge us to come in with confidence—"so that we may receive mercy and find grace to help us in our time of need" (Heb. 4:16).

For heaven's sake—yes, literally—our number-one life project must be to learn to "worship God *acceptably*, with reverence and awe, for our God is a consuming fire" (Heb. 12:28, 29, emphasis mine)!

7

The morning after the meeting at the Hartfords' house, Joanna stood around in the kitchen sipping orange juice and feeling restless as a cat. She looked at Lady Magdalene, a limp bag of fur sleeping in the sunny window bay. Well, she amended her thoughts, as restless as Lady Magdalene in heat.

Joanna couldn't stay in the house and think—not this morning. Julia was coming to houseclean, and anybody's presence would interrupt her thoughts. Why didn't Julia show up, then? For the perfectly good reason that she wasn't due for another ten minutes.

Joanna drummed her fingernails on the kitchen counter. She looked down; a little nail polish was starting to peel. Anything to kill some time. Passing her messy desk (no use getting into that; she couldn't concentrate), she went up the stairs and into the master bath. A good orange-y polish color would pick up her spirits. Was she too restless to hold steady? With care she painted her nails, sitting on her boudoir bench and keeping an open tissue under the field of operations. . . .

The doorbell rang. "Come in, Julia! I unlocked the door for you," Joanna sang out.

She stood at the top of the stairs with her hands spread out. "I can't come down for a minute; my polish is wet. How are you, Julia?"

Without waiting for an answer—"I left a lot of ironing for you to do, including some sprinkled table linens in the refrigerator. Julia, there's a spot on the lower front of the love seat in the living room—the white linen slip cover. And you won't forget to water all the plants?

"I'm going out this morning, and I don't know exactly when I'll be back. You'll find plenty of leftovers for lunch. Take any phone calls, but I can't promise when I'll return them.

"Julia, will you dig my car keys out of my purse for me?" She came down the stairs. "It's not chilly still this morning, is it? . . . I'll be on my way. If I'm not home by the time you leave, lock the door after you."

The Mercedes glided smoothly out into the sunshine. Joanna steered with the flats of her fingers and gingerly turned the radio knob. The news came on.

"At a meeting of the California Coastal Commission yesterday, a series of compromises appear to have opened the way for the development of the Irvine Coast, between Laguna Beach and Corona del Mar. . . ."

Damn, said Joanna. If those stupid commissioners let in tourists and riffraff, there'll be no place left for us to flee to. The quality of Newport Beach must be maintained at all costs. I'm going to write them a letter. . . .

She turned downhill toward the coast and found her way to a familiar parking space. Locking the car, Joanna picked her way over the grass and down a steep path to the rocky shoreline. The tide was fairly high, but it was waning. Joanna was ocean-wise enough not to get caught on a rock in rising tide.

With the roar of the surf all around her, she climbed the slippery, wet surfaces to her very favorite perch, her "thinking place." With her two hands she steadied herself and reached for and climbed into a rocky saddle, just her size, and settled herself in with her legs straddling.

Whoosh! A giant wave crashed nearby and bathed her bare legs and tennis shoes in its cool spray. Oh, I'm so happy here, thought Joanna. I love you, ocean.

She looked out at a distant rocky outcropping rising darkly from the restless whitewaters. Joanna focused her eyes until they could distinguish between the grey of the wet rock and the grey of fat seals sleeping on its surfaces.

Whoosh! Another wave sprayed her, closer than the last, and Joanna thought, When I love you, ocean, why don't you love me back? You couldn't care less if you knocked me right off my think- ing place. You are beautiful, fascinating, and cruel.

Her mood darkened as her mind flicked to David. She had thought that David was a pond—placid, never-changing—and she'd discovered he was an ocean! She had thought that he would always be there—and she'd discovered that he could rage forward, hurting her, and then recede out of her grasp. Joanna shivered.

Well, she'd come here to think about last night at the Hartfords'. . . . Such a surprise! When she had stepped into the Hartfords' house, she'd stepped into a world which was totally un- familiar to her. Could this be a correct simile?—it was as if, in her church experience, she'd been viewing Christianity fuzzily, through unadjusted field glasses, and last night Roger and Clare had ad- justed the lens for her.

Last night it seemed as if she had clearly seen both love and wisdom in action. She stopped to ponder those two things.

Love. The people she knew said pleasant, witty, fun things, sometimes thoughtful and important things, but things definitely adjusted to the ears of the hearers. Behind backs, the story might be different. Her friends weren't, on the whole, actually *loving*. They played to the galleries, as she and David did.

What was the basic difference, last night? The people seemed truly concerned for each other. Roger had spent a lot of time pre- paring, to help those people grow. He cared about them. And they prayed for each other so sincerely. . . . It seemed to be love at work.

And wisdom. David's and Joanna's friends were not stupid. They were informed, and they were sharp. They represented thoughtful, stable, wholesome, Christian, Orange County Republican conservatism. They were the hope of America, Joanna had always thought, standing against the Midwestern blue-collar unionists, the Eastern intellectual radicals, and all the rest out there hatching their liberal plots to take the world over for socialism, Communism, and humanism. What more should anyone do, than fight as they did in Joanna's crowd for God, country, and all that was decent and good?

But last night, eight adults began by asking the Holy Spirit for wisdom. That seemed to put them onto a different level right away. And their studying seemed to be not to bolster their own viewpoints but to probe into that which was outside of themselves, beyond themselves, higher than themselves. They were like little children—truly humble and curious. They searched with seeming earnestness, not trying to ratify anybody's platform but to study what *God* had to say.

All Joanna knew about the Bible was the usual Sunday school stories; there had seemed to be a lot there last night that she'd never delved into.

She was intrigued by those people. But then, she tried to picture herself as one of them. If she sat around reading her Bible all the time, her tennis might get rusty. Maybe she couldn't drink any more, or have any fun. Her friends would probably cool off. Would she have to give a lot of money away? Would she start wearing polyester and doing her own hair? Her lip curled.

The surf was receding, and the waves were slapping the rocks further out. She looked down beyond her feet at their final foaming releases, and at their swirling and sucking as they withdrew.

Then she looked up into the warm sunshine, and watched the gulls wheeling in the blue air, and heard their squealing cries. One of them made a sudden dive, and came up out of the water again with a fish in his mouth.

It doesn't make sense, she thought.

Gulls catch fish. Women lose husbands.

Her mind seemed burdened with questions. Which is more important—conservatism or piety? She had thought her religion was enough: a popular, political Christianity accepted by even the news media of America. Vaguely, she sensed that the spirit those eight people represented was something different: a mind and heart broken before God and shaped by the Holy Spirit.

Must she eventually make a choice?

Her eyelids felt heavy, and she untied the sweater around her shoulders, bunched it on the rock before her, and pillowed her black head on it. Soon she was almost dozing. Occasionally thoughts flickered by:

Maybe I will become the most outrageously attractive and sought-after single woman in Newport Beach. . . .

David will come back quickly; things will get better; no one will ever know. . . .

I think the Irvine property investment is about to mature; I could live on that for a year, at least—with or without him. . . .

Melissa, Steve—are you grown up enough to handle your father's walking out? . . .

Whatever happens, I will never leave Newport Beach. He may; I won't. . . .

David! David! Your curly red-brown hair, the feel of your body—Come back! Come back! . . .

The gulls glided around her, slanting in the sun. Surf crashed and sprayed and retreated, endlessly, endlessly. If anyone had been standing on the rocky coast, with binoculars they could have spotted fat seals dozing on a far-out rock, and a slim woman dozing on a nearer one.

8

The hours of early morning are at their darkest, and Joanna is having a bad dream. Alone she walks in the middle of a great, floating, unstable valley. The valley floor is sticky and hard to maneuver on, but she picks her way, looking for David. He doesn't seem to be anywhere around, and she begins to cry. The air seems heavy, and pushing her down onto the stickiness.

But suddenly there is a presence at hand. It's Hank Jones; she recognizes him. Hank is a fellow Joanna has known almost forever, a sophisticated, smooth-talking man, always ready with a laugh, a pat, a cool word for the occasion. Hank's hair is almost as black as Joanna's, and his tall frame stoops just enough for a certain glamor. Several times married, he's single these days, and lives maybe thirty miles away. Lots of Joanna's friends know him and admire him. . . . Hank, what are you doing here in this valley?

He seems dreamily near, comforting her with pats and squeezes, and murmuring in his wonderful bass voice, "Let me come in to you, Joanna. I've always liked you. . . ." She doesn't see him as much as feel and sense him; he seems to be in the shadows—enticing, exhilarating, naughty.

He offers her something to smoke. She pushes his hand away, and notices that the hand she's holding is forming a vulgar sign. She tries to act playfully shocked, and works to rearrange his fingers. Try as she will, they are locked into position, and strong.

The struggling makes Joanna increasingly nervous, frustrated, and anxious. Summoning her composure, she tries to explain to him: "Hank, you're just not my type. I'm basically a nice person, and I really prefer David, but I don't know where he's gone. ..."

Her eyes search the horizons of the great valley, and her feeling of desperation grows: "David! My big redhead! I don't want him, I want you! Come get me; he's too close. *Hurry*, David—!"

Joanna's sobbing woke her up, and she sat up in the big bed, panting and miserable.

Oh, what a dumb, stupid dream! What made that stupid Hank Jones come into my mind? The impression of him overwhelmed her again: dark, smiling, quiet, and dangerous. She lay back down, turning from one side to the other.

It's not the room that's dark, it's my mind. This is stupid! Switching on the light, Joanna was temporarily comforted by the Baroque mirror, the familiar luxury of her surroundings.

Enough of that, she told herself—smoothed her sheets, found a new, cool spot on her bed, switched off the light and lay down again.

I remember reading that depression is always connected with loss, she thought. Sometimes it's imagined loss—like worrying that others don't like you and you've lost your status. Or projected loss—like worrying you might get cancer and lose your health. Or real loss—as when a husband walks out! I certainly have every right to feel depression.

Now that I've analyzed it, that should make me feel better. ... She waited. ... It doesn't. Oh, David! Come back, come back!

Time passed. She writhed. She pounded her pillow. She tried different positions. Would the night never end? Eventually she turned on quiet music and drifted into fitful sleep.

Joanna woke again in early daylight. The continuing music reminded her painfully of the past hours: that stupid dream about Hank, her thoughts about depression, the struggle with sleeplessness.

I've got to fight my way out of this immediately, she said grimly. I'll confront David. Forget my pride. I'll plead with him to come home. She swung her legs out of bed. I'll bet that's what he's waiting for!

Excitement prodded her, but Joanna bathed and dressed carefully. If he was on his usual morning schedule, she still had over an hour before he would leave for his office.

What would an attractive, appealing wife wear? Bright colors for morning cheer, soft fabric asking to be touched, an understatement of jewelry. . . .

Presently, in front of the magnificent mirror, she looked. Her soft, two-piece jersey dress shaded from gold to orange in smudged, undefined swirls; it had cost her a fortune, and she was glad she hadn't resisted it.

Then Joanna carefully critiqued her face. The black hair was almost straight, but blown-dry full and bent to frame her thin face in the latest mode, exposing gold hoops at her ears. Thank God I had it done yesterday, she thought. Her makeup was perfect, particularly her beautifully shaped mouth, but her eyes looked tired. All her skill at blending mascara to lift their outer corners couldn't hide the fact that she'd had a bad night.

In the kitchen Joanna poured a glass of orange juice; she must have energy for what she needed to do. Then with soft leather bag slung over her shoulder, she backed the Mercedes out of the garage, by remote button shut the garage door, and started for the nearest motel.

Would it be the right one? It was conveniently close. She tried to compose sentences that would quickly, appealingly bridge the gap between them—the terrifying gap, now, of both space and time. David, I had to find you. I had to make the first move, because it's been my fault. I'm so lonely for you. David, I love you. And for the children's sake, we must be a family. Can't we try again?

Tears so blinded her that she pulled the Mercedes to the side of the road to compose herself, and dabbed her makeup with a tissue. Then she proceeded to the motel.

She knew this one well. Whenever there'd been more guests than their spare beds could handle, they'd put the overflow here. Joanna moved to the desk and asked if a David Heston were registered there. Yes, he was indeed. And could she use a house phone to call him? She could, and she did.

The phone rang—and rang.

Joanna began to chill with fear. Is he burying himself in longer work hours? Or is he . . . sleeping elsewhere?

The little coffee shop was tucked around the corner. It was full but quiet, except for the clatter of dishes. Businessmen were breakfasting and reading papers—but David was not among them.

To the phone again; perhaps he'd been in the shower. The ring in her ear repeated itself monotonously: gone . . . gone . . . gone . . . David! What are you doing?

Joanna never remembered the drive home, but as she parked in the garage, feeling her chest tight with agony, the phone was still repeating in her ears: gone . . . gone . . . gone. . . .

No, it was her own phone! She sprang out of the car and caught it in the kitchen: "Mrs. Heston—"

Words poured from the receiver—words of chatty familiarity: "Joanna, this is Betsy. We haven't settled the tennis thing this week. When do you want to play? I can make it any time in the mornings. What do you think?"

Suddenly Joanna was furious—at David, at herself, at the awful timing of Betsy's call. Harshly she snapped into the phone, "Betsy, set up your damn tennis game with somebody else this week, all right? I just can't do it."

"Well!" came Betsy's surprised retort. "Excu-u-se *me!*"

The words seemed flung in Joanna's face, and she riled all the more. "Betsy—" thrashing about in her spirit, totally irritated, she heard herself saying loudly into the phone, "Betsy, you're a great gal, but bug off, okay?"

She crashed down the receiver and stood in the middle of the kitchen, mouth hanging open in horror. Betsy will think I've been drinking. What *is* the matter with me? Is it the bad night, and the disappointment of not finding David? Or am I losing my mind?

9

In spite of his words, when David left Joanna that Sunday afternoon he had no intention of staying away very long. Indeed, he checked into the closest motel right away, thinking there would be no time wasted when he'd have to come back semimonthly to care for family finances and other matters. For many years he had loved Joanna, even though through increasing frustration; and all he thought he needed was a little space in his life to think, to plan his strategy, to woo her again.

An end room in the motel was available; it looked great. The big walk-in closet held his clothes comfortably; he approved of the ample bath with its huge, thick towels; and he felt at home in the handsome bedroom with its balcony turned inland to view those restful, gentle Corona del Mar hills.

Darkness was falling. After settling himself, he put on his swimsuit, slung one of those thick towels around his big, freckled shoulders, and went down the back stairs to the pool.

The lights had come on, with tiny hanging lanterns dancing in the night air like fireflies. The water was a blue-green emerald of magic, and he was alone. He knifed his body cleanly into it, felt the surprise of cold and then the exhilaration of body adjustment. He swam strongly downward and around underwater for a while, then exploded out onto the surface, blowing and snorting. The sky was partly starry and partly covered with the night-clouds weathermen call "coastal fog," which often hover over the California coastline at night and evaporate in the morning sun. David floated on his back, looking around. Not bad, not bad. Or as he and his friends would say, not too shabby, not too shabby.

He swam a few laps and then lingered, dawdling, until a couple in swimsuits emerged from the motel. Then he lifted himself deftly out, toweled a bit, and dripped his way up the back stairs again.

The shower was positioned for a man, and spacious. He turned it warm, then cold, and stepped out feeling marvelous. If this were Japan, he thought, I'd have a man's kimono and slippers to put on, to go get a bite of supper. Well, he slipped his big frame into shorts and a tee shirt, put thongs on his bare feet, and scuffed down to the coffee shop.

A quarter in the slot for a Los Angeles *Times*, and he sat reading all kinds of inconsequential things, as he went through a bacon-lettuce-and-tomato and several cups of coffee. A few people were around, but their voices were low, and the Muzak was soothing.

He scuffed his way back to bed, repeating—as he climbed in and tested it approvingly—not too shabby, not too shabby.

David got his big frame comfortably between the sheets, and he let out a giant sigh, as if to expel everything bad that the earlier part of the day had brought. The quiet, the aloneness, was good, already.

And not until then did he think to himself in surprise—I've hardly thought of Joanna since I got here.

10

The business was jumping, and almost totally absorbing for a while. Quickly David settled into a routine between motel and office. It was nothing to drop off laundry and dry cleaning on the way. And he'd been used to so many business meals in restaurants that he hardly noticed he didn't have a "home," except to feel released to concentrate on the deals that seemed to be popping all over.

But there were a few blank spaces. He stayed away from church, found that sexy movies and television didn't do him any good, took lots of cold showers and played tennis like a wild man.

("Dave, you're absolutely going to kill me," panted Herb, his best friend, with a face furiously red under his thatch of dark hair. "Will you please make up with Joanna? I haven't beaten you once since you split!")

I'm getting lean and mean, thought David, as he climbed on the scales he'd bought and noted that he'd slid down another pound. Women were making me soft. Look at that flat belly!—as he surveyed himself naked in the mirror. But then he looked further down. Am I up to being a celibate for long? he wondered.

Gradually, as time passed, David began to feel itchy, guilty, restless. He had moved out to have time to think, and the new life was whipping along so fast, he hadn't had the time at all. He was no farther along in getting his head together about his marriage than when he'd left.

Suddenly he knew what he had to do: take a long weekend at a hotel in San Diego (sometimes they'd gone there for vacations) to get away from the Newport Beach rat race.

It was Wednesday when he dropped into the office of Hal, his partner, and opened his mouth to broach the subject.

Hal beat him. "Dave, man, the call just came through from Merrill Lynch. This is going to be the hottest thing we've ever handled." He threw up his hands like a cheerleader. "Oh, cool, cool, cool! I bet there's a coupla million in this first part of the deal, alone."

"Gosh!" David excitedly jingled the keys in his pocket. "We beat out Dudsy-baby and Akron and probably others, too? Did you nail down a date to talk details?"

Hal shook his head. "The Big Man they assigned to clinch it with us has somep'n else going, and we're next in line. We'll phone every day to—uh—gently keep ourselves in the foreground.

"It's about to break, Buddy, it's about to break!" He was doing the cheerleading thing again.

"Hal, ol' buddy," David leaned over the desk. "I'm glad I have a thoroughly competent partner, because it probably won't break 'til next week, but the fact is, I'm gonna take a long weekend Friday. I'm gonna clear out at noon and come back Monday noon. Nothin' should happen at all 'til I get back, but if it does, give me a call. I'll be in San Diego and I'll give you my number. I'll be back in a flash—competent, cool, casual, quick, ready to sew that baby up with you."

"Hey, wait, Dave, not this weekend! We've gotta be on the spot if this thing breaks!"

"Look, once it does, we've got a month's close work putting it together. There'll be no time then. It's now or who-knows-when, and I need to go have myself some quiet and think about Joanna. Gotta do it, Hal, gotta do it."

And he was gone. By Friday evening, a good dinner under his belt, David found himself strolling alone along a beach.

Who am I? he asked himself. Where have I come from; where am I going? And Joanna fit in my past, but does she fit in my future? Have I outgrown her? (Now, there was a nice, ego-building thought.)

The evening winds lapped the waves upon the cold sands, and ruffled his hair.

He thought about his Irish Catholic parents in Long Beach, where he'd grown up. They'd been good, hard-working people, and David appreciated his home, his high school, his old friends.

By college years he was no longer going to mass, which he knew disappointed his parents. When he began trailing cute, black-haired Joanna around and going to Protestant church with her, his parents were somewhat comforted. Any church was better than no church.

As the Joanna romance developed, he discovered he hadn't gotten involved in just a girl—but in a whole family! Joanna's huge clan, Armenian by blood and by passion, had fled to Pasadena from the Old Country when they could escape the terrible Turkish persecution two generations before.

Joanna particularly adored her grandmother, and could hardly wait for David to meet her. She turned out to be a tiny, bent, old-world lady with dark skin, white wisps of hair, and gorgeous love and light shining out of her brown eyes. Mostly she sat by the window of her little Pasadena cottage, reading her big Armenian Bible ("Breath," she said the name of it was, in the Armenian tongue), and lifting her head occasionally to pray for passers-by.

She was tiny, but her spirit and will were huge; thanks to Grandmother, neither her children nor her children's children ever stopped going to church. It would have been unthinkable to defy Grandmother.

As Joanna brought David, this sandy-complected Irish Catholic, into her family circle, he discovered another hard fact of life: no one in the clan had ever married a non-Armenian—not uncles, aunts, cousins, brothers, or sisters. They looked at this intruder first with cool reserve, some with outright hostility.

And when Joanna and David were married in her lovely church in a lavish, fashionable wedding, an aunt and two uncles refused to come. All the rest, particularly cousins, brothers, sisters, and in-laws were there; the youngest generation in America was getting more tolerant.

The early married years were spent in Long Beach, where David worked in his father's box-manufacturing company, and then, on the sudden death of his father, found himself running it. But always Joanna and David had had their eyes on Newport Beach down the coast; and when his father's estate was settled, they put their inheritance money into Newport Beach real estate.

Marvelous! Its value inflated so steadily that eventually they moved to a modest home in Newport (the price seemed ghastly), where they could keep a closer watch on their growing investments. Increasingly, David gave more time to land acquisition and development, and on his fortieth birthday he sold the box company and was through for good with commuting to Long Beach.

"The three considerations in buying real estate are location, location, and location," Newport Beachers told each other knowingly, saying it every time as if it were the first. And so, when an opportunity was ripe, David worked a "deal" on a prime sea-view home on the hills of Corona del Mar, and settled his Joanna and growing Stevie and Missie in new luxury. In so doing, he joined the "in" ranks of the financial entrepreneurs of Newport Beach, who quietly play their cards right and gallop along financial miles ahead of current American inflation.

But with new successes (in Newport Beach no one ever says "rich"; people are only "successful"), Joanna seemed to become more and more uptight.

(David slopped his way through a surging, chilling wave underfoot, and thought about it.)

Fashion seemed to become her lord, and doing the "in" things, her master. She eschewed extra calories as though they were poison. Her house had to be perfect; the cars had to be right; everything had to be approved by "them." The "them" were all the other Newporters who, like themselves, advanced through life eyeing each other sidewise to check labels on clothes, memberships in clubs. His poor Joanna! She was totally caught up in it, and one look at the strain in her eyes showed that she was paying for it. "Success" had made her dry, tight, preoccupied. Their sense of companionship had evaporated.

Well, what to do? It was easier to assess the problem than to solve it.

Saturday and Sunday passed with no insights in view. On Monday morning, feeling trapped and despairing, David roared his little Fiat up the San Diego Freeway to Newport Beach and the office.

11

Hal was on the phone as he walked in. His voice was controlled, and casually perfect. It told David the call was important. David hung his suitcoat on the copied-antique bentwood coatrack and sat down, straightening his vest and tie. Full of curiosity, he fiddled with the leaves of the potted ficus beside him.

"Sounds good, then." Hal was all velvet. "We'll get on it from here. Thanks much."

He hit the receiver to its cradle and leaned toward David, wide-eyed and grinning. For a breathless space of time he said nothing.

"Come on," urged David, grinning Hal's contagious grin. They were both tense, ready to break into little-boy giggles.

Hal stage-whispered, "You won't believe it." He licked his grinning lips. "Dave, we've hit the big time."

Another silence.

"Come on!" shouted David.

"Soon as you left Friday—you hadn't been gone five minutes—ol' Merrill Lynch puts me on the phone and says Marcus Weatherhead's got a cancellation, and can we meet him *now*. Marcus Weatherhead! How ya like that name?

"You were just startin' down the freeway, Buddy! Two hours 'til you got there, two hours for return trip—no way. You're off the scene. You're zip.

"So I handle it myself. Marcus Weatherhead and I get together at his place. (Wo-o! You should see that office!) Three hours Friday afternoon and two hours this morning, and the thing is sewed up, Dave! I kid you not. A straight two million contract for the Mission Viejo deal, probably Oceanside after that, more to come...."His hand waved at the portfolio on his desk, and again came his awed stage whisper: "Dave, take a gander at this deal!"

Before he sat down, David looked out the glass expanse behind Hal at a blur of Newport office high-rises and green areas. Joanna, Joanna, he was thinking, suddenly sad. For so long we worked together to reach this point. Will you share the financial fruits with me? Would it all just make you tighter, harder than you are now?

His heart grew bitter. Maybe this will just make alimony easier.

12

Anne: Joanna and David don't know it (and in this they're typical of millions), but both of them have a terrible sickness. They have the disease of self-centeredness, of self-preoccupation. *Joanna worships Joanna, and David worships David.* And as long as they do, they can never worship God, and they can't even truly love each other.

It would be impossible. As far as God is concerned, at this point in Joanna's life, that "adoration" study in Roger's group won't be anything more than a mental exercise for her.

They don't know yet that Christian married love isn't two people absorbed in each other; it's two people together absorbed in God! It's when they love him more than they love each other that they can really learn how to love each other!

When missionary C. T. (Charlie) Studd became engaged, he made up a little poem that he made his future wife promise she'd repeat every day:

> My Jesus, I love Thee;
> Thou art to me

> Dearer than ever
> Charlie can be!"

This is the freedom we all long for. This is release. This is when living gets fun!

Ray proposed to me with Psalm 34:3: "Oh, magnify the Lord with me; and let us exalt his name together" (KJV)! To that I said a joyful "yes"! Believe me, we're not much, especially me, but maybe we've been too scared of the alternative not to try to put God first.

From the start, although Ray was a student and we were poor, he insisted on our giving God at least a tithe (one tenth) of our income. In exchange for the sacrifice of our doing without, God has poured back his amazing supply.

We offered ourselves several times to mission boards, saying we'd go anywhere we were needed—to hard places others didn't want. We were refused for medical reasons, but God has since made us healthy travelers with the whole world as our ministry.

The way to "up" is "down"! Every time we've humbled ourselves before him, he's raised us up. And the process continues. In our truly feeble way, we volunteer to be buried seeds, and he keeps making our lives sprout!

"Adoration" is your lifting up *him*. Moment by moment, it's the growing habit of practicing his presence, admiring and worshiping him in your conscious thoughts. *You* can't be on the throne of your daily thoughts; *he* must be.

And "adoration" as a larger lifestyle grows out of that. It shapes itself in weekly public worship without fail, in yielding to his lordship in all decisions. *You* can't be on the throne of your life patterns; *he* must be.

In both cases, if you give God the lead, he will take you to paths of fulfillment, achievement, and joy you never dreamed of! But you have to lower yourself and surrender to him totally.

You simply can't worship both God and yourself. Neither can I. We must be down; he must be up. It's that simple.

The world around you constantly encourages you to be occupied with—and fascinated by!—yourself. The talk is all about self-esteem, self-concepts, self-image. People get rich urging you to discover the real "you," to realize your full potential, to accept yourself, know yourself, love yourself, be your own best friend, look out for number one.

All this occupation with "self"—what do you think; is it the newest idolatry?

Constance Rosenblum put her finger on Joanna's and David's basic problem, I think, when she wrote in the *New York News* that "narcissism is on the upswing:"

> Top social scientists are calling [it] the major disorder facing Western society today. Analysts say patients with traditional Freudian neuroses are being replaced by the New Narcissus—a self-centered, self-serving creature so preoccupied with himself and his problems he has no energy left to relate to others.[5]

We first saw Joanna so occupied with her looks, her clothes, her life, her inner thoughts, that she hardly knew David occupied the same house with her. She had little energy left for him.

Rosenblum describes a person afflicted by this new mental sickness:

> [He] is totally self-absorbed, with an exaggerated sense of self-importance. He craves admiration, but puts others down. Though charming, he has few emotional contacts. He flourishes best in highly impersonal settings, like bureaucracies, which put little premium on personal attachments.[6]

I have a feeling that God is giving me something important to say in this chapter. We're trying so hard today to worship both God and ourselves, and it seems as if we're failing pretty badly at both.

I have inside of me a hundred temptations to make it my chief goal to be some super-Christian (even worshiping God better than anyone else!), and all the voices around us all would "egg me on" to do it:

> The new alchemical dream is: changing one's personality, remaking, remodeling, elevating, and polishing one's very self . . . and observing, studying, and doting on it. For generations this was a luxury reserved for the very rich. But by the sixties, everyone with a few hundred dollars could buy, for example, a week of self-improvement at a trendy place. . . .[7]

What's back of it all? I don't know, except that the reason Lucifer, a chief angel, was thrown out of heaven long ago was that he wasn't satisfied with his status and said, "I will make myself like the Most High. . . ."The implication was, "I don't need to recognize God as my Creator. 'I will make myself'; I will be self-made." So God expelled him and changed his name to Satan.

But the answer isn't to grovel and think we're nobodies! A "poor self-image" is sick, too! It's denying what God's grace has done for us. When God tells us over and over to be "clothed with humility," humility isn't self-negation or self-depreciation. Great guns! If you're a Christian right now as you read this (if you've accepted Jesus Christ as your Savior), whether you know it or not, already you are—

1. Chosen by God (1 Thess. 1:4);
2. Redeemed by Christ (Col. 1:14);
3. Justified freely by his grace (Rom. 3:24);
4. Reconciled to him (Rom. 5:1, 2);
5. Forgiven of all your sins (Col. 2:13);
6. Condemned no more (Rom. 8:1);
7. Made eternally perfect (Heb. 10:14);
8. Qualified to share in the inheritance of God's children (Col. 1:12);
9. Freely given his glorious grace (Eph. 1:6);
10. Made the righteousness of God (2 Cor. 5:21);
11. Made near to him (Eph. 2:13);

12. A child of God (John 1:12, 1 John 3:3);
13. As a child, an heir (Rom. 8:16, 17);
14. Released from the law (Rom. 7:6);
15. Rescued from the dominion of darkness (Col. 1:13);
16. Now light in the Lord (Eph. 5:18);
17. A citizen of heaven (Phil. 3:20);
18. Seated with him in heavenly realms (Eph. 2:6);
19. A member of God's household (Eph. 2:19);
20. Born of the Spirit (John 3:6);
21. Baptized by the Spirit (1 Cor. 12:13);
22. Sealed by the Spirit (Eph. 1:13);
23. Indwelled by the Spirit (1 Cor. 6:19);
24. Glorified (Rom. 8:30);
25. Given all fullness in Christ (Col. 2:10);
26. Blessed with every spiritual blessing (Eph. 1:3);
27. In God (1 Thess. 1:1);
28. In Christ (John 14:20);
29. In the Spirit (Rom. 8:9)[8]—

—all that already, by his omnipotent decree, and much more! He's really taken us off the ash heaps, as 1 Samuel 2:8 says, and set us among princes!

I don't understand what all of these mean (do you?). I just know that each one is going to be far more wonderful than we can imagine.

One time someone asked a Christian, "If I accept your Jesus Christ, what will happen to me?"

The answer was, "You will stumble upon wonder after wonder, and every wonder will be true!"

You know, when Christians are untaught about the highly exalted position they already have in Christ, they fight for self-esteem. But when they see where and who they truly are, they can afford to be humble! We don't exalt ourselves; we must not exalt ourselves. He's already done it for us!

A. E. Whitman says it so well: that if I try to love myself, God loves me more. That if I try to defend and protect myself, God already defends and protects me totally. That if I exalt myself, God exalts me far more. And that it's ridiculous for both of us to be doing it!!

Oh, what an exalted spot he gives us! As he called John in Revelation 4:1 to "come up here" into heavenly realms, so he has given each of us believers the status of owning a private card which admits us at any time into his very presence. But when we realize where we are, and look around—up in that high, shining atmosphere of God, we discover that everybody around us has fallen flat on his face (Rev. 7:11)!

Those who realize how *up* they are are the ones who will fall *down*—in humility and worship and adoration.

13

But everybody's asking the question, "Who am I? Can't I discover my true identity? Don't I have the right to know?"

Thomas Howard recently wrote in a magazine article about this curiosity we have to know ourselves. He points out that neither dogs nor even angels seem to be puzzled by the fact *that* they are, let alone *who* they are. Only recent humans seem to be all engrossed in the Big Question.

But Mr. Howard asks, "What is it that God seems to spend his time trying to get across to us in his Word?

> What does [God] say? Thou shalt love the Lord thy God. . . . Follow me. Be kind. . . . Be faithful. . . . Blessed are the pure in heart. . . .
> "Yes," [you say] "yes of course. All that. But is there a word about my self image? Can you tell me how to come to terms with myself? After all, I must find out who I am before I can do anything else."

Maybe this thinking explains Joanna's exaggerated consciousness of her mirror. Her constant inspection of herself may reveal a deeper, unconscious anxiety about "Who am I? Who am I? I must know. . . ."

Mr. Howard answers Joanna,

> Must you? *To him that overcometh will I give a white stone, and in the stone a new name written, which no man knoweth saving he that receiveth it.* Your identity, perhaps, is a great treasure, precious beyond your wildest imaginings, kept for you by the great Custodian of souls, to be given you at the Last Day when all things are made whole.

Isn't that intriguing? He goes on to say,

> This acute self-consciousness and self-scrutiny that has been laid on us by the sciences of the last hundred years may be a burden beyond our capacity to manage. Our ids may be there, so to speak, but they are none of our business, just as the fruit in Eden was there but was not healthy for us to chew on.[9]

Mr. Howard defines "health" as "that state of affairs in which our insides are working quietly and efficiently so we can get on with the job." He believes that when we get psychologically sick, then some probing and introspection may be temporarily necessary to get us back to health. But he writes that our general task is to keep our eyes on our faithful Custodian and trust him—not to spend our time and energies "pawing into the safe," trying to uncover ahead of time his own secrets about our true, fabulous identities!

Check out that wonderful Song of Solomon, God's most beautiful love poem. In the admirations of the lover, there is almost no mention of self at all. He is just absorbed by and thrilled by all the charms of the one he loves.

When lungs are healthy, they breathe lots of air and are easily expanded. And their owner stands tall—and can accomplish a lot—without being conscious of his lungs at all. So, my friend, when you are full of the Spirit of God, your life will be almost unconsciously healthy, and able to expand enormously! Be personally encouraged!

But think about it: adoration brings us to the unspeakable difference between God and man.

We are not mini-gods. We are not God-clones. Only God is God! And the Bible's final words tell us to adore and worship him alone (Rev. 22.9).

Charles Spurgeon said,

> I hardly know how to describe adoration. Praise is a river flowing joyously in its own channel, banked up on either side that it may run toward its one object.
>
> But adoration is the same river overflowing its banks, flooding the soul and covering the entire nature with its great waters; and these not so much moving and stirring as standing still in profound repose, mirroring the glory which shines down upon it, like a summer's sea of glass; not seeking the divine presence, but conscious of it to an unutterable degree, and therefore full of awe and peace, like the Sea of Galilee when its waves felt the touch of the sacred feet. . . .
>
> It is the eloquent silence of the soul that is too full for language. . . .
>
> This should be the frequent state of the renewed mind.[10]

Renewal Is Born in Desperation

14

Joanna was wiping off her brown Mercedes. It showed every speck of dust! She hated all the dusting it required, but she'd always said the deep, rich brown color was worth it. This time she *over*-wiped; she polished vigorously, trying to relieve the tensions within her. She'd been running on the beach; her body was sweaty and fatigued, but still she rubbed.

Finally she threw down her rag and went inside and climbed the stairs. She ripped off her Adidas and sweatsuit, stepped under the shower, and began to cry. Her voice rose to a wail above the sound of the water.

"David! David!" she sobbed. "You dummy! Where are you?" Anger and grief fought within her, and she cried louder.

"Oh, oh, oh!" She banged her fists against the tile. "You stupid, damned idiot! I want you, I need you! You jerk, David!" She washed off her runny nose under the shower and helplessly let the sobs convulse her.

"David! David!" she cried. "I'm going crazy living in this stupid house all by myself! I can't stand it! What do you want me to do, invite in some stupid live-in?" Her aching body told her it wouldn't be too bad an idea, and as her sobs subsided, a crazy line flitted through her head; it had the intonations of a card shark's: "Pick a man, any man. . . ."

She stepped out of the shower, sniffing, and David stood in the bedroom. *David stood in the bedroom.*

"What are you doing here?" she trembled.

He offered vaguely, "I'm supposed to be at work."

Joanna stood there, not knowing what to say or do, and then he was around her, all over her wet body, dampening his shirt, his trousers, and she was as eager for him as he was for her.

> May your breasts be like the clusters of the vine,
>   the fragrance of your breath like apples,
>   and your mouth like the best wine.
> May the wine go straight to my lover,
>   flowing gently over lips and teeth.
> I belong to my lover,
>   and his desire is for me.
>
> * * *
>
> Come, my lover, let us go to the countryside,
>   let us spend the night in the villages.
> Let us go early to the vineyards
>   to see if the vines have budded,
> if their blossoms have opened,
>   and if the pomegranites are in bloom—
>   there I will give you my love.[11]

. . . Joanna lay in bed listening to the click of the door downstairs, the familiar sound of the electric garage door going up, the Fiat starting up and backing out, and the sound of the door returning to its place. As usual, by the time the door was down, the sound of the motor could no longer be heard.

"David, you dummy," she said out loud, and grinned. She reached over for a decorating magazine on the night stand, flipped the pages for a while, and then unexpectedly went into a deep, contented mid-day nap. . . .

The phone was ringing. "Hello?" groped Joanna.

"Joanna? This is Susie," said a voice.

"Yes?" said Joanna.

"Susie Carlson! From the Bible study group!"

"Oh—oh, of course, Susie! How nice of you to call!"

"Bruce and I just wondered if you and David could come over for dinner tonight before the Bible study. It's just one of those spur-of-the-moment things, but I made some really great soup today, and we thought it would be fun to get to know you two better before the meeting. Does it sound okay? Do say yes!"

Joanna's normal inclination would have been to add her cheerful bubbles to all that this conversational bubble-machine was already making, but from the first mention of David's name an alarm had gone off in her heart, and she was fully awake. Was David coming back at dinner time, she wondered? He had made no commitment.

"Susie," she stalled, "we've already got a dinner date tonight."

"Oh, weren't you coming to Bible study?" asked Susie. "I thought you promised to bring cookies."

Joanna was verbally thrashing around. "It's an early dinner commitment because David has to go back to the office and work tonight. Yes, I'll be there. I know I promised to bring cookies. I'm really sorry we can't come over for some of that wonderful soup, and you were a dear to ask."

"Maybe a week from tonight, then." Susie's bubbles would not turn off. She's getting obnoxious, thought Joanna, as she wrapped a housecoat around her and went down to put brownies in the oven.

The afternoon hours stretched out longer than the rays of sun slanting over the ocean and the gentle land. David was seldom out of her thoughts. Will he quit work early to come home again?

Joanna picked daisies from around the pool area, put them in a happy yellow vase on the breakfast table, and decided to make a simple supper for two. The smell of brownies baking made her almost feel as if all were well again; the nostalgia of it reminded her of all the years David and Stevie and Missie and she had been in the house together—not this house, but others. . . .

She went upstairs and put on some chocolate-colored velvet pants, a chocolate silk shirt, and a long rope of pearls. In front of her Baroque mirror.

The brownies were done; the smell diminished; her anxiety grew. Supper was ready. . . .

Supper was getting dried out from waiting. . . .

Supper was ruined, and so was Joanna.

She dialed the kitchen phone. "Clare, I've got a headache, and I just can't make it tonight," she said.

"Oh, I'm really sorry. . . ." Clare seemed to be stammering.

"Can you survive without my brownies tonight?" asked Joanna.

"Oh, of course, we'll miss *you,* not just your brownies," said Clare.

"Suddenly I feel stupid about this," said Joanna. "I'm standing right here looking at these brownies; they're all baked and ready. Why don't I just swing them by your house and then come on home?"

"Oh, Joanna, you shouldn't if you don't feel well—"

"Well, I baked the stupid things, and if they sit around here, I'll just eat them, and I mustn't." Her mind was made up. "I'll just slip them by," she said.

Soon her slim, brown-clad figure was inside Clare's door, and she laid the big silver tray of brownies on the dining table. Roger poked his head out of the kitchen.

"Joanna," he said, "Clare's putting her face on, and she's left me alone out here, and I don't know how to turn down the coffee maker. Can you help me?"

"Of course," said Joanna—and discovered the creamer and sugar bowl were also set out waiting to be filled. . . .

And before she could get out of the kitchen again, Susie and Bruce were filling the doorframe, saying, "Hi! Hi, everybody! Joanna, your outfit is darling. . . ."

72

And what was she to do but settle down in the group for the evening?

Roger was a beautiful man, she thought—just the kind she wished David were. He was earnest and steady and *reliable.* She had always thought David was reliable, but boy, was she wrong.

There was a lot of talk about "Priority One" tonight, of making Christ first in our lives and worshiping and "adoring" him. Roger led them in a study of Colossians 1:15–19, to demonstrate the matchless qualities of Christ.

"For by him all things were created," they read, and Joanna wondered why he hadn't done a better job of making David?

". . . And in him all things hold together," said verse 17. Did that include marriages, she asked herself? Was David really delayed at mealtime, and was he coming home tonight? In her mind she pictured his coming, and she planned what she might say or do. . . .

Roger was saying, "Joanna, is there anything we might pray about this week for you?"

"Oh," said Joanna, fumbling around, "I've been asked to serve on a committee at church to redecorate the social hall, and you can pray that I'll know whether to do it. I'm pretty busy right now."

"All right," said Roger, and the group bowed for prayer. Several of them prayed for wisdom for Joanna concerning that committee. They prayed so earnestly and lovingly, she felt absolutely foolish. She was thankful that Clare had assured her she need not pray out loud in the group.

Then it was over, and she pressed the leftover brownies into Clare's hands to be frozen for another meeting, took her empty silver tray, and hurried home. The house was dark, except for the customary night lights.

David's half of the garage was empty.

David's half of the bed was empty.

15

Spring seemed late to Joanna, even though spring in Corona del Mar is a February event. The chill in the air kept the budded trees from opening up, and the chill in her heart produced the same effect. She seemed enclosed, encased, unresponsive, remote even from herself. Three weeks had passed since David's departure. She'd stayed away from church; she hadn't mentioned anything in her letters to the children; she hadn't told her family (Grandmother? heavens, no!); she'd gone to the discipling group, but stalled off that aggressive Susie. Joanna felt frozen, immobile.

She was aware that David had come one evening while she was with the Bible study group and had written checks at his desk. Does he know about my group? she wondered. Or did he expect me to be home? Her heart turned hot and cold over the possibilities.

Joanna's own desk was as messy as ever. She couldn't seem to settle down to correspondence or chores. Time seemed to pass, but there was no accounting for it. She burst into tears occasionally. She was lonely, but afraid to reach out. Clare had phoned twice, and Joanna had stiff-armed her: "I'm okay, Clare, Don't worry, I'll keep coming to your group. Yes, I missed church because I went out of town to visit my uncle. . . ."

How long can I stall? How long can life be in a holding pattern?

Joanna put on her sweatsuit and Adidas and went walking. She thrust her hands in her pockets and tossed back her black hair and looked around at the world.

God, I think your world is a mess. It looks so good on the outside, and when you get inside, it's so crummy. O Lord, I know it's because of sin. I know things would be better if people followed you. Maybe things would be better for me, too. Roger and Clare seem happy. . . .

She had rounded a corner, and there was David's car! It was parked in front of Frannie Simmons's house. She knew that house very well; Bill, her decorator, had also done that one, and had gotten Frannie Simmons's permission to walk her through to look at it.

But Frannie Simmons herself was enough to look at. She was a bosomy, blonded divorcee with lots of new money and a reputation with the men. When Joanna had first met her (she'd never forget!), Frannie had gold polish on her fingernails and toenails, and was wearing at-home pajamas of black see-through chiffon. *Cheap!* thought Joanna, and felt sick as she saw Bill ogling and handling her. . . . Oh, yes, that was Frannie Simmons's house without question. *And David was there.*

She changed direction and stonily walked home again. Her emotions seemed to be freezing over. A knot was locked inside her chest, but she didn't cry.

She stormed upstairs, showered, and made up her face very carefully. She put on her taupe suit with a striped silky blouse, slipped her legs into dark stockings and her slender feet into her highest heels. She checked in front of her beloved mirror, and added her long rope of pearls and a huge pearl ring.

Lastly, onto her lips she smoothed a marvelous new lipstick she had just discovered. She scrutinized her mouth for a moment in the mirror, smiling, pouting. *Sexy!*

David can't do this to me. I'm not trash.

Joanna backed out the brown Mercedes and began to drive. For half an hour, at least, she had known where she was going. She guided the car smoothly through the quiet, late-afternoon light, avoiding the freeways filled with husbands commuting home to their wives. . . . She clenched her teeth in cold anger.

The drive to Hank Jones' was only thirty miles. . . .

Inside the city limits of his town she stopped at a pay phone. She'd brought along his number; Hank worked in investments out of his own home. Now she could only hope that he was there.

"Henry Jones speaking," announced the crisp bass voice. Hank, if you only knew how familiar your voice is, since that dream!

"Hank, this is Joanna Heston."

"Sweetie!" The velvet tones raised half an octave. "What are you doing? Are you over here in my neck of the woods?"

"Yes," she said breathlessly. "Actually, I'm in a phone booth in town, and I'm here for the sole purpose of finding out if you are free to take me to dinner."

"Joanna, you have just made my day. I'm totally at your disposal."

"Come on," said Joanna. "You must have had something planned—"

"Whatever it was, I can't remember. Where are you?"

Joanna told him.

"Then let's have our date on the opposite side of town, so that while you're driving over there, I can be putting a little after-shave behind my ears. Do you know Westfall's?"

"No," said Joanna.

Hank gave her the address and some directions, and she put the receiver back in its cradle. For an instant her conscience gave the slightest twinge, but she ignored it, slipped into her car, and drove on her way.

Now the in-city traffic was really heavy, and it took her more than half an hour to get through the heart of town and out the other side. When the city had definitely waned and become even thinly residential, there was Westfall's. It was not a restaurant. It was spread out and quietly plush—obviously a cottage hotel.

Her mind was steel. For some reason she ignored the attendant and parked her own car, then came inside, stepping quietly over the heavy carpet. "Dining room" said the sign. And there was Hank, looking more darkly handsome than ever. Oh, how good was the feeling of a man's embrace again!

"Joanna, I've missed you so. I thought you'd never come back home to me again." Light teasing was perfect for the occasion.

"You're goofy, Hank. . . . I hope you have lots of money, because I'm hungry."

"Joanna, I phoned Fort Knox, and they're standing by in case I run out. The world is yours; at least, my share of it is yours. Let's have a party."

He guided her to their softly lit table, and she felt a little faint with excitement. "You order for me, Hank. Driving through rush hour traffic took all my adrenalin."

He ordered the drinks very carefully, and the food, as if the chef were to feed the queen of the world.

He looked at her long and hard as they ate, and he never mentioned David, nor did she.

A little combo had started to play, and they stood up to dance. "I will surrender to his arms as if there was no other man in existence," Joanna told herself. "This is good. I will enjoy every minute of it. I will be soft and feminine and yielding."

Hank danced closely, smoothly. Even in her high heels her head was only to his shoulder, and sometimes she put it there, and he kissed her hair. When fleeting thoughts of David came, she thought of Frannie Simmons, and a little flame of self-justification burned uncomfortably inside her. Mostly, she thought not at all.

The combo pounded its makes-you-want-to-dance music. They

were good together; it was really fun. They danced a long time. Finally they were laughing and breathless, and he said to her in his wonderful bass voice, "Come on."

This was the moment of interest. He took her hand, and they walked together through the shadows of the grounds. We're so compatible, Joanna insisted to herself; this could go on forever. She blocked out thoughts of her dream.

From out of his pocket came a key. "Well, how about this?" said Hank, in mock surprise. "I wonder if it fits a door?"

They were close to a cottage nestled in the shrubs, and he tried the lock. "Well, what do you know?" he marveled, and led her inside without turning on the light.

She heard the door shut softly, and his hands were cupping her face and neck. Then they stroked her thick hair as he moved closer, and simultaneously his wet mouth and his body were laid against hers. Joanna closed her eyes. She was almost relaxed against him.

Hungrily his hands began to explore. . . .

Then she stiffened. This wasn't David. She couldn't breathe. She stepped back, and in the dim light saw the door handle. She must get it open; she must get across the grassy areas; she must find her car quickly; she must get her key out of her purse and unlock the car door. . . .

She flung herself into the seat and started the ignition. She had a surprising thought that no one seemed to be chasing her—but she didn't stop to find out. She backed the car out and sped away down the highway, away through the towns, away through the countryside. She was shaking, she was crying, and she opened the window partway to get some air. The moonlight was brilliant, and she began to sob, "Thank you, Lord; thank you, Lord; thank you, Lord; thank you, "Lord. . . ."

She had escaped that horrible, stupid thing. Suddenly it seemed *totally* stupid to her. "*Stupid*, Lord—!" she gulped, out loud. It was the only word that seemed to fit. "Oh, how stupid! How *stupid*—"

Then she realized she was driving twenty-five miles per hour over the speed limit. She slowed down, and went on talking: "O God, please calm down my mind, as well as the car, before I have an accident. Dear Lord, you have snatched me out of something dreadful tonight. I am your child, but I almost did something really stupid. Oh, dear Father—"

Suddenly she had to smile. She was praying out loud at last! Clare would have been proud of her.

16

Sunday morning Joanna knew she would be in church again. Ever since that almost-stupid night, she'd been strangely sympathetic to the pastor. She was understanding his longing for renewal in his congregation; sin was on every hand, and everyone was either on the brink of disaster or already into it! She was frightened of herself. She reread the Bible passages the small group had studied. She thought how deep Roger and Clare were, and how burdened as the pastor was burdened—and she wondered if Susie and Bruce and Fred and the girls in the group "got it" at all.

Suddenly she shared the longing—that God would wake up the people to their sinfulness and give them a breakthrough to reality. She thought of all the phoniness and garbage that would have to be cleaned out of the lives she knew, including her own. She wondered how renewal could happen in the church, and thought somehow that it could happen if people really realized they could meet God there, instead of just each other. She thought how God must be waiting in the wings somewhere for the people to discover that possibility. And then she remembered that old painting she'd seen of Christ standing, knocking, at a door all overgrown with vines. . . .

She thought her own heart must be that door, but she didn't know what to do about it, except to start going to church again.

When Sunday morning came, Joanna was walking through the patio fifteen minutes earlier than usual. A few of the old cronies were already there.

"Jo-*anna!*" cried Susie from the crowd. "All *right!* We thought you were getting to be a pagan, for sure. Here, have a cup of caffein. Your suit is just *adorable.*"

Joanna smiled, "I really apologize for missing. Well, here I am again, anyway. I think I'll just go on into church. Thanks, I'll skip the coffee."

And so she slipped inside, and nobody had had a chance to ask about David.

The organ was playing. An usher nodded and greeted her; she accepted a bulletin and found a seat.

God, are you here? she asked silently. You're so holy—I can see why you might bother with Pastor John and Roger and Clare, but I don't know how you could want much to do with *me.* She felt Hank's hands upon her, and her eyes stung and moistened. Oh, no, not my mascara. . . .

The hymn book was before her. She opened it at random:

> Oh, for a closer walk with God,
>   A calm and heav'nly frame,
> A light to shine upon the road
>   That leads me to the Lamb![12]

It sounded terrifyingly sweet and simple. Lead me back to the Lamb, Father, she said humbly. I lost him somewhere, years ago. I don't know what a "frame" is, but I'm sure mine isn't calm and heavenly.

She blew her nose.

The opening hymn started out with the "Lamb" again!

> Lamb of God, our souls adore thee,
> While upon thy face we gaze;
> There the Father's love and glory
> Shine in all their brightest rays.
> Thine almighty power and wisdom
> All creation's works proclaim;
> Heaven and earth alike confess thee
> As the ever great I AM.

How incredibly beautiful, thought Joanna! Had other hymns spoken of his face, his love, his glory, his power, his wisdom—and she hadn't been paying attention? When she got to the last two lines, she wistfully pictured herself kneeling with all the throngs of heaven and earth to acknowledge him.

Pastor John was continuing his series of sermons on renewal, and today he was preaching from Mark 14:3:

> While [Jesus] was in Bethany, reclining at a table in the home of a man known as Simon the Leper, a woman [John identifies her as Jesus' friend, Mary] came with an alabaster jar of very expensive perfume, made of pure nard. She broke the jar and poured the perfume on his head.

"Mary poured out a very expensive gift," said the pastor. "And that's what worship is.

"We worship as we give back to him of that which he has given us—and it must be in some way proportionate to his giving, or it's just plain silly.

"God says to us, 'I love you,' and with that he 'graciously gives us all things'—Romans 8:32. If we say, 'I love you, too, Lord' and offer him a dollar bill, he must say, 'You gotta be kidding....'

"Mary gave so much that everyone around her was shocked. But Jesus didn't say, 'Now, Mary, I understand your heart, but you take back half of this. After all, you've got your expenses. God helps those who help themselves. He wants you to use your common sense, too.'

"No, he said, 'I tell you the truth, wherever the gospel is preached throughout the world, what she has done will also be told, in memory of her'—verse 9. And twenty centuries later, I'm here still fulfilling that prediction.

"Ladies and gentlemen," said Pastor John earnestly, as he leaned over the pulpit, "are you really learning what it means to worship God? Oh, how I long for you to! Are you learning what it really means to tell him you love him?

"His love was sacrificial; yours must be, too. Any love that is not costly is phoney."

Joanna blinked back her tears. I wish I'd loved you well through these years, Lord, she prayed, but my life's been too crummy; I've spoiled everything; you're too high above me; it's too late. . . .

She tried to keep sobs from gurgling in her throat.

C Stands for Confession

17

Anne: "Joanna."

Joanna: "What do you want?"

Anne: "May I interrupt again?"

Joanna: "Why didn't you tell me how miserable all this was going to be?"

Anne: "Joanna, my life is miserable, too, sometimes. And maybe so are many of the readers'. Hopefully, as we work together, we can help them."

Joanna: "It's too painful. I'm backing out."

Anne: "Joanna, you can't! What would I do if my lead character backed out in the middle of the book?"

Joanna: "Hah! You're just trying to use me. I won't be used."

Anne: "Dear friend, do you remember your first conversation with me? This was all your idea, and you volunteered. You offered yourself, and you promised that you were ready for whatever came."

Joanna: "How did I know David would walk out? How did I know I'd be hit with all this dumb realization of the futility of my life? It's humiliating! It's embarassing! I've had nothing but pain in this book!"

Anne: "Joanna, the aim of this book is renewal—yours, mine, and the reader's. Stick it out, Joanna. Be a model to remind me that God can renew me, too—and to remind the readers of the same thing.

"God works through pain to bring glory! All of us have to understand that. God's fabulous treasures aren't bought with cash and credit, slapping down a contract on a bargaining table and scratching a signature and a date. They just don't come that way!

"Our Lord Jesus suffered, too, to show us the way. He suffered first and most—to purchase for himself glory in our eyes (Phil. 2:5–11). First the pain, then the prize.

"'Come, let us return to the Lord,' says the prophet Hosea:

> He has torn us to pieces,
> but he will heal us;
>   he has injured us,
> but he will bind up our wounds.
> After two days he will revive us;
>   on the third day he will restore us,
> that we may live in his presence (6:1, 2).

"Do you catch something here? It's as if the shadow of a cross is falling across these words. God is totally involved in our suffering, as we will be totally involved in his ultimate triumph. The two processes are inseparable."

Joanna: "Do you mean I'm not even through suffering?"

Anne: "After 'adoration' comes 'confession.'"

Joanna: "Whatever it is, I don't want it."

Anne: "I don't blame you a bit, dear—not a bit. I'm going through a thing or two in my own life, too.

"But, Joanna, there's a third party here, you know. Maybe the reader is going through something hard; did you ever think of that?

"How about a three-way pact? Reader, put your hand in here with Joanna's and mine. She doesn't mind joining us, even though she's fictional and we're real. Let's pledge that we'll hang in there together, and see by the end of this book if God has worked through the 'baloney' and brought glory to our separate lives.

"His aim for his children is always renewal. The crunches he puts us into to bring us low are only to lift us up! If we are patient in suffering and look to him, the end for us will be fantastic! You know what Ethel Waters said: 'God don't sponsor no flops!'

"Then are we all up for a great conclusion? All *right!* Then we can talk about confession for a while, but know that happier stuff is coming!"

God's great men often confessed that they were small and unworthy. (See, for instance, Judg. 6:15,16; 1 Sam. 15:17; 1 Sam. 18:18,23; 1 Kings 3:7-10;—there are many more.) Don't worry, they weren't groveling around with poor self-images; they were great because they were humble. And God could afford to exalt them, because all the glory and credit remained his.

"Therefore," said Paul, who was such a great apostle, "I will boast all the more gladly about my weaknesses, so that Christ's power may rest on me" (2 Cor. 12:9).

That seems going too far. How could he "boast gladly about his weaknesses"? Because he understood how gladly God forgives! He knew that when we rush to God with our confessions, God rushes to us with his forgiveness! It's like the prodigal son turning homeward—and the father running to meet him.

I'm learning in my own life that constant, instant confession is the means to continual health, to unbroken communion with the Lord and with others. As often and as quickly as I say "I'm sorry," God or the offended one says, "That's okay!" And when I keep short accounts on my sins with continual confessions, then acknowledging my sins doesn't crush my ego and totally embarrass me. I can open up gladly about my weaknesses—and expect glad forgiveness!

Joanna isn't there yet. Her sins have stockpiled for so long, it's going to be a most traumatic event for her to unmask. When

Christians have "followed Jesus afar off," and habitually faked and lied their way along to keep their sins covered up, renewal doesn't come without great effort and great agony. But when the old habits are replaced with the new habit of instant confession, renewal becomes a continuing way of life.

Not long ago Ray and I had an all-day conference in Ventura, about a three-hour drive up the California coast from our home. It was to begin at nine o'clock in the morning, so before daybreak we were getting ready to leave. Ray was already in the garage when I decided we needed a little fruit juice in our tummies before we left, and I drank some cranberry juice and poured a glass for Ray.

I started through the door into the garage just as he decided to come back in and hurry me up! Collision! Cranberry juice all over my white wool suit! I was a mess!

Eventually we were on our way, with both of us angry. Ray was seething because I'd made us late in the first place with the dumb juice idea. I was seething because I'd had to change to an old green suit, and because Ray didn't appreciate my attempt to be thoughtful!

We were mad at each other the whole trip up the highway, including breakfast in a coffee shop along the way. We were even mad at each other through the first hour of our speaking together in the conference!

But by the end of the first session, the Word of God in our very mouths had broken us down. When we put the people into discussion groups, we could hardly wait to turn to each other and say, "I'm sorry! I've been such a pill! Please forgive me—!" Actually, by that time it struck us both as funny! We both had felt pretty foolish, and the confessions were an enormous relief.

> If we confess our sins, he is faithful and just and will forgive us our sins and purify us from all unrighteousness. If we claim we have not sinned, we make him out to be a liar, and his word has no place in our lives (1 John 1:9,10)

We can easily confess the sins of others. All those awful people out there in America, or elsewhere, need revival. This attitude makes fussing Christians ("America is going down the tubes"), and it purges nobody's sins at all. "Don't grumble against each other, brothers," says James 5:9, "or you will be judged. The Judge is standing at the door!" David expressed the only attitude which God promises to honor: "Cleanse *me*... wash *me*..." (Ps. 51:7, emphasis mine).

Yesterday I said some things on the phone to our daughter Sherry that I need not have said. She took it as an unjust criticism, and immediately we had a problem. The rest of the phone conversation was definitely unhappy, and I hung up groaning. For a while I rammed around town, doing errands and feeling miserable. Then I knew what I had to do.

I bought a basket of pink chrysanthemums. I showed up at Sherry's front door, looking and feeling foolish. I ate dirt. I apologized for my big mouth. I only wish I'd thought of one other touch: to put a card in the flowers saying, "Single-handedly, I have fought my way into this hopeless mess!"

After hugs and tears came a glass of iced tea and some fun, and all was well again. Whew! Relief! Now I can look Sherry in the eye again and know we're still best friends: "Therefore confess your sins to each other and pray for each other, so that you may be healed" (James 5:16).

And don't think that basically we're really fine, that it's only around the edges that we still need a little polishing up. Don't say to the Lord or to anyone else, "Forgive the little thing or two I did...." Little? Our sins are enormous! They put Jesus on that bloody cross!

The Publican pounded on his chest and cried, "Lord, be merciful to me, a sinner!" This man, went home justified rather than the religious Pharisee. When he took the low position, God could lift him up.

Lots of veteran Christians live relatively ineffective lives because of unconfessed sin. There are actions in their past they've never dealt with, so they get hardened and "professional." Yet God is "faithful and just," and he would cleanse them quickly if they'd only confess!

A little bit ago, when we read 1 John 1:9, we were two verses away from a terrific insight on this business of confession, in 1 John 1:7:

> If we walk in the light, as he is in the light, we have fellowship with one another, and the blood of Jesus, his Son, purifies us from every sin.

This is an amazing truth. It doesn't say that "God is light," like other passages. It says that he is "in the light." How is God "in the light"? He, too, is exposed. He has made himself knowable to us. Then we are also to "walk in the light," in exposure, with God as our Model. We're to be "the real us"—no faking allowed!—knowable as he is knowable. Then we're like him!

When one person is in the light and another is in shadows, there's no fellowship. Most church congregations are partly in darkness and partly in the light. The continual revival in the East Africa churches has brilliantly illustrated for us that when we meet around Jesus, we're gathered around the light. Then we're all in the light together, all confessing our needs and joys and sorrows together.

When we stay in the light, sins are confessed as soon as they occur, and we stay purified. Oh, it feels so good personally—and it feels so good relationally!

I remember when Ray was speaker at Wheaton College's Spiritual Emphasis Week one year, and God gave us revival, a campus-wide renewal that changed our own lives as well. During that week a girl asked for an appointment to talk to me.

"Mrs. Ortlund," she said, "eighteen months ago I surrendered my life anew to the Lord, confessed my sins, and I thought I was off to a fresh start. But eighteen months later, I can't see that I'm any different. So what good did it do?"

At the moment, the newspapers were full of New York's city-wide garbage strike. Pictures showed alleys and streets piled high with overflowing cans of garbage and trash. "Dotty," I said, "what if New York's garbage and trash hadn't been collected for the last eighteen months? Confessions and fresh surrenders to the Lord are like garbage collections. My goodness, I have to reconsecrate myself to the Lord every other day, at least! I don't know about you, but I really need to confess my sins and have them disposed of and start fresh with the Lord several times a day!"

And we can't "walk in the light" and despise a fellow Christian. It's impossible! "Loving our brothers" keeps us in the light—in the condition of being continually open people. We no longer "hide" from each other in any way, and it's our great joy to lift each other up. Oh, what happy "community" this makes!

One last word about this, a great word of comfort. First John 1:9 tells us to confess our sins—but how can we confess them all? Part of our very sinfulness is that we're so dull, we don't understand much of our own sin. In the light of God's perfect standard of holiness, we are much worse than we think!

> Joseph de Maistre once said he did not know what a scoundrel's soul might be, but he knew well what the soul of a good man consisted of, and it was horrid. It is the whispered confession of us all.[13]

But God is so kind. When we "confess our sins"—whatever sins we *do* become aware of—he is "faithful and just, and will . . . purify us from *all* unrighteousness"! As you confess what you know, he will also forgive what you don't know. Partial confession produces total forgiveness. Praise the Lord!

> Jesus, Thy blood and righteousness
> My beauty are, my glorious dress;
> 'Midst flaming worlds, in these arrayed,
> With joy shall I lift up my head![14]

"*T*ake with You Words. . . ."

18

Joanna walked out of church that morning slowly, waiting as those in the rows behind her moved out into the aisle. Everyone seemed thoughtful and uncommunicative, and she felt that way, too. The organ postlude seemed louder than usual; it made a good excuse not to engage in small talk.

But at the rear of the sanctuary, there were Susie and Bruce coming on her left, and the bubble machine was going full force.

"Joanna, isn't he ter*rif*ic? Wasn't that sermon just too *much*? See what you two have been missing lately? How's my favorite couple, anyway? I swear, you two look so cute together!"

Joanna opened her mouth to meat-grind out the usual baloney—and then she realized that David was in the crowd on her immediate right! Of course Susie had supposed that they were together. Her face was burning. "Thanks, Susie" was all she could think of to say.

And there was David to deal with. He looked as surprised and awkward as she. He also looked taller, handsomer, better. His reddish brown hair was waved exactly right, though his faintly freckled face seemed pinker than it should.... She felt as self-conscious as a high schooler on a first date.

"Good morning," he said quietly.

No words seemed right. "Good morning," she answered lamely. Now they were side by side in line, moving out to greet the pastor at the door.

"How are the Hestons this morning?" he smiled as he shook hands.

"Fine," they lied in small voices, and went out on the steps in the sunshine.

He asked, "How are you, Joanna?"

Oh, dear Lord! What was she supposed to say? I am an embarrassed woman, afraid to face society because my husband has left me. I'm suddenly alone, and I feel incompetent. I am lonely, I feel threatened, I am furious, I feel rejected, I feel frustrated, I feel—she couldn't say even inside her heart "still desirous of you." And yet she stood there, looking at him, twisting the straps of her purse, yearning.

He waited, and she hadn't said anything.

"It was a dumb question," he apologized. Still he stood there. "Do you want some brunch?"

"Yes," she whispered.

"Leave your car in the lot," he said. "We'll come get it afterward."

She eased herself into the little Fiat, and he shut the door for her. God, she prayed, you know I'm on new ground; I never lived this day before. I don't deserve anything at all, but are you going to give me back David? (He had swung in beside her and was starting the engine.) Lord, I don't want to blow it. First, before I say anything to David, I want to tell you I want the kind of renewal, and the kind of love for you, that Pastor John was talking about. That's first, Lord. And then, please give me back David.

"You're a quiet lady," he said.

"Yes, well, I guess I haven't had anybody to talk to, and I must
have forgotten how."

"Poor baby," he said—and was it mocking, or was it tender? She
couldn't tell.

"What's new?" he asked, and her face burned. Pieces of
memories flashed before her: first David's car in front of Frannie
Simmons's, then Hank's hands. . . .

"I'm not starting off very well," he said awkwardly. "I just don't
know what to say to you."

"David," she blurted out, "I'm trying to get closer to the Lord. I
don't know how to describe it, really, but I started going to a
discipling group with Roger and Clare Hartford. There are eight of
us, and we've been studying ACTS—A, C, T, S. They stand for
adoration, confession, thanksgiving, and supplication. . . . It sounds
silly, telling you."

"Go on," said David. "I'm listening."

"We study the Bible each time, to see what it says about these. So
far we've just studied 'adoration' and 'confession,' and, honestly,
David, each week I've felt more—more *awed*. It's just a new
atmosphere—I don't know. How can I describe it?

"I've always had certain things I could count on for status; you
know, my clothes, my car—even my husband—to give me security
and acceptance with people. These days I'm being shown different
values. God is wonderful, and he is important, and I feel as if he's
been waiting for years for me to find this out."

The little Fiat had parked in a spot overlooking a harbor filled
with yachts. When she paused he hopped out, came around and
opened her door, and they began strolling along the rail beside the
water.

"Are you hungry?" she apologized. "I've probably talked enough."

"Just wait a moment, and I'll turn in our name at the restaurant,"
said David, and disappeared.

Soon he was back. "Twenty minutes 'til our name's called," he
said, "so go on."

"David, I've stumbled into a new world. It's not just churchgoing; it's not just the external parts of life; it's not just going through religious motions. It's taking seriously the Bible and Jesus Christ and all that we've been giving lipservice to.

"He's really there, David! And he's really wonderful!" She turned to him, the ocean breezes blowing a cut of her black hair across her forehead. They leaned over the rail.

"Roger makes us memorize verses out of our *Living Bibles.* Listen to this—Hosea 6:3: 'Oh, that we might know the Lord! Let us press on to know him, and he will respond to us as surely as the coming of dawn, or the rain of early spring.' Isn't that beautiful?"

She hurried on, to press her point. "You know all the courses I've taken over the years—history courses and aerobic dance and speed-reading and typing and even comparative religions. They all put facts into me, or skills, and they were great.

"But this group is different. The Bible is getting inside my heart. God is speaking to my *life,* my attitudes—does that make sense, David? And when I look up and begin to get a glimpse of him, and how holy and amazing he is, and discover that he loves me—he *really loves me,* Joanna Heston—

"Oh, David!" she cried. "I'm embarrassed that I was such a poor wife to you! It was all my fault! I was so totally selfish and self-centered. I'm full of pain over it. I wasted so many years of *your* marriage! I wasn't putting contributions into it *for you,* making it meaningful and worthwhile and even fun for you! I didn't know God could get me outside myself, to learn to love you and give to you. I still don't know much about it!

"But, you know, I keep thinking of that little song:

> Jesus loves me;
> This I know,
> For the Bible
> Tells me so!

"Because he really loves me, I can be totally forgiven by God! I can start again! It's wonderful, David!"

Her voice, her attitude seemed as fresh as the ocean breezes playing around her.

But David looked puzzled. "You've always believed that, Joanna. What's so new about that? You've always believed in the Bible, and in God's forgiveness, and all the stuff you're telling me. So what's so new? Are you into some kind of cult or something, and you don't even know it?"

Joanna was confused, seeing the old Joanna through David's eyes; and for a moment she wondered if she was getting pumped up over nothing, or if Roger and Clare were subtly brainwashing her into something strange. Her mind fished around for a memorized Bible verse to cling to, and she felt so inadequate in the Scripture!

"David," said Joanna, "there's a lot I don't understand yet. But the greatest commandment is, 'Love the Lord your God with all your heart, and with all your soul, and with all your strength.' " (Even as she verbalized God's Word, she felt him renewing her and putting words in her mouth.)

"This is the God of my childhood. *He* isn't new, but *I'm* getting new. I'm just discovering that the reason my life has been so dull and unproductive and meaningless is that I've made no attempt to love him in the way he asks me to."

They were not far away from where the little Fiat was parked, and Joanna retrieved her notebook.

"Listen, David," she said, "I can't say it well on my own. Let me read you some of my notes:

God told Abraham in Gen. 12:1, 'Leave your country; get away from your father's house. . . .'

God was saying to Abraham, 'Leave your old habits, your routines, your lifestyle—all that determines your life and holds you prisoner, all that which seems normal only because it's so familiar to you, and everyone else does it.

'Come to me!' he says. 'Start fresh! Shuck off the unworthy. Let me rearrange you, put you together.'

This takes time. Put yourself under him a good while every day. Sit at his feet. Let him teach you, correct you, do what he wants to do with you.

"I'm starting to do that, David," she said earnestly. "I've been a Christian since I was little girl, but lately he's been becoming real to me.

"Look, this is how it was even with the apostles. They'd been with Jesus for several years. But after they saw his death and resurrection and ascension into heaven, and they began to get the picture of who he really was, then everything was changed. They were full of joy, and they were continually worshiping him and praising him! It made all the difference."

David was quiet during their brunch together. As he watched her, her beautiful olive skin seemed to glow. And as she leaned forward to talk, there was a new sweetness and decisiveness about her. Joanna, involved in what she was saying, didn't notice that he seemed insecure. It didn't occur to her that he might be threatened by this new Joanna.

He guided his little Fiat back to the church parking lot, and when he stopped, he kept the motor running. Quickly he hopped out and opened Joanna's door. And awkwardly he guided her elbow as she moved toward the Mercedes, touching her gingerly as if he were somehow dirty.

Then he was gone, and Joanna sat dumbly at the wheel of her car.

"Lord, I want him," she whispered. "Did I scare him off? Was I being stupid?"

Joanna—and Anne

19

Anne: I'm learning about confession, too, as I write this about Joanna. She is new in the experience of total surrender to the Lord. It's been my life-attitude for many years. But it's always time for a fresh start. I've been discovering how much pride there is in my heart, and how much I need to have washed out of me! (Here comes my "pain" part, right?)

My books have sold very well. They've given me status among my peers in this world, just as clothes, etcetera, have given Joanna status among hers. And so I've gotten comfortable and smug in that security, and I needed God to draw me out of that, and to lead me to new humility and commitment.

Around me here in Corona del Mar are lots of joggers. Morning, noon, and evening they're on the streets and the beaches, identifiable by their running togs and their strained expressions! Always they divide into two categories: those who discover that using unused muscles *hurts*—and quit—and those who press through the pain barrier to become fit and sound.

I'm pressing through a new pain barrier. At a time in life when the world says I should "have it made," I'm experiencing new sandpaperings to expose my inner carnality. Oh, have I been inwardly complaining, lately! I thought I didn't deserve it at all—until in gathering book material on "confession" I came across these old notes of my own:

> Complain as little as possible of the wrongs you have to put up with. Self-love magnifies all that, makes the injuries worse than they are, and keeps us totally upset.
>
> Nothing in Scripture ever tells us to "demand our rights." God is the true Judge, working behind the scenes to continually justify those whom he has already justified, and to continually hassle and ultimately punish those he has "condemned already" (John 3:18).

As I copied this quotation just now, I looked up John 3:18 to see again its context. Here are some verses following it:

> Everyone who does evil hates the light, and will not come into the light for fear that his deeds will be exposed.
>
> But whoever lives by the truth comes into the light, so that it may be seen plainly that what he has done has been done through God (vv. 20,21).

Anyone close to me these days might sense some overconfidence in me. That would quickly become obnoxious, and then I'd be open for criticism. The solution is for me to confess it first, as soon as I see it in myself, before others can judge me for it.

I'm writing this on a Tuesday morning. Tomorrow, when I'm in two weekly small groups, I plan to tell them what I'm seeing in myself. I can hardly wait! Psalm 32 says how "blessed" it is to confess sin, and describes the joy that immediately comes. Confession is like taking a bath!

Oh, I know it will be embarrassing at the moment. But I know, too, that God will share with me the awkwardness of my confession.

One time when Ray and I were watching our son Bud play football for Wheaton College, Bud was hit hard and suffered a shoulder separation. As soon as he came off the field, Ray was down at the players' bench, and a news photographer caught a remarkable shot. He got Bud bent over in pain, and his father above him, also bent over in pain—their profiles and blond heads almost identical. That's the way our heavenly Father suffers when we suffer.

But what's the path to being "lifted up" in the Christian life? (We all long for that.) James 4:6,7,10 says it:

> God opposes the proud but gives grace to the humble. Submit yourselves, then, to God.
> Humble yourselves before the Lord, and he will lift you up.

There it is. That's how we get lifted.

My last book, *Children Are Wet Cement*, [15] tells about three methods for effecting changed behavior in others (for them I'm grateful to Sally Folger Dye):

1. The shape-up method ("You shape up, or I will see to it that there are certain negative consequences");
2. The pull-up method ("I will set for you goals, and help you achieve them; and when you do, I will reward you");
3. The lift-up method ("I will expose my own vulnerability; I will share your weaknesses; I will lift you by making myself lower than you are").

God's been teaching me about these, even since I finished that book! For instance, I've discovered that these three methods have been God's methods for seeking to effect changed behavior:

1. He began with the shape-up method: "You stay away from the fruit of a certain tree, or I will see to it that you die" (Gen. 2:16,17). That method failed.
2. Then he used the pull-up method: "I will give you certain boundaries and goals (the Ten Commandments, all the Mosaic law), and I will help you achieve them; and when you

do, I will reward you with the Promised Land, with health, with prosperity, and every good thing." That method failed. (Of course, when we speak of "failure" with God, we know his ultimate purposes will still be carried out.)

3. So he used the lift-up method: he "made himself nothing, taking the very nature of a servant, being made in human likeness, and being found in appearance as a man, he humbled himself and became obedient to death—even death on a cross!" (Phil. 2:7,8).

Yes, he made himself lower than we are—becoming "sin for us"—this fabulous One who never had committed any sin (2 Cor. 5:21, my paraphrase)! And this is why the Father could lift him up and exalt him to the highest place (Phil. 2:9–11). He became a model for us, even in leading us out of sin, by showing us that the way to Up is Down. It was, even for God—wonder of wonders!—and it is for us.

Confession is at the heart of this lift-up method. By it we not only lift others but ourselves! It's just plain smart, then, to confess. When I defend myself, others will be quick to judge me. When I judge myself, others won't—I got there first (Rom. 14:10–13).

In a forest fire there's a place the flames don't touch; it's the place that the fire has already burned! The fire's already done everything it could do, and therefore that spot is actually a place of protection and safety.

Our confessions are what firefighters call "backfiring," deliberately burning an area in advance before the fire can get to it. We protect ourselves when we confess! We are agreeing with others' potential—and correct—judgment of us, and then, from that moment on, we can never be justly accused again. Before judgment fire got to us, we jumped in and confessed!

Oh, this is a good word for me, struggling toward godliness! I love it. It makes me happy. Listen to this great word written centuries ago by Francis de Sales in that ancient classic, *Introduction to a Devout Life:* [16]

Let us not be disturbed at the sight of our imperfections, for *perfection consists in fighting against them.* And how can we fight against them without seeing them, or overcome them without encountering them? *Our victory consists not in being insensible to them, but in refusing them our consent;* now to be displeased with them is not to consent to them. . . . *We shall always be victorious provided we do but fight* (emphases mine).

Joanna has come to the point where confession, at least to those closest to her, is her most urgent need. She has gotten a glimpse of who God is; she is beginning to incorporate the acts, the attitude, the atmosphere of "adoration" into her life. And immediately on beginning to see who he is, she begins to see *who she is.* Confession is then imperative.

She must get into the light, as he is in the light, in order to have true fellowship with him and with other believers. She can't hide any longer in the shadows. Her unanswered question from the time David left until now has been, "How long can I stall? How long can life be in a holding pattern?"

Now Joanna sees that with confession she can break the pattern and move forward. But when, where, how, and to whom?

Ross Foley writes that it's important for us to confess not just to anybody, but to a few people who are truly significant in our lives. He says that this will liberate us from fear and guilt as little else can. And he points out that this is not only biblical, but it's "been practised in the finest epochs of church history."[17]

He tells about the "Great Awakening" of the eighteenth century. From a Moravian named Peter Bohler, John and Charles Wesley learned the principle of meeting in small groups for sharing and confession and prayer. Their resulting instigation of "class meetings" was the "method" which became worldwide "Methodism"! In these class meetings, five to ten people were to gather each week. After an opening hymn and prayer, they were to go around the circle, each one telling his temptations since the time of their last meeting, and how he was delivered! This kind of continual confession to meaningful friends as a way of life, was so powerful, it became God's tool for the revival and renewal of the whole English-speaking world of that time.

It may well be that no society has ever been transformed as deeply as eighteenth-century Great Britain was by this confession-in-small-groups movement. Never have so many people stayed so purified and so healed, and therefore free to shape their government and societal framework. On the western side of the Atlantic, the shaping of the United States' form of government was all part of the fruit of this godly, powerful movement.

Why should open confession of sins to a small, meaningful group of friends be so potent? Well, everybody needs a way to deal with personal sin. Today the "method" is often to keep it bottled up inside until we're ready to explode, and then to rush to some professional counselor.

Herbert Mowrer writes,

> If "secret confession" to priests and psychiatrists had a really good record of accomplishment, we should be glad to be spared the embarrassment of having the "ordinary" people in our lives know who we are. But the record is *not* good, and, reluctantly, many people are today experimenting with *open* confession of one kind or another.
>
> When you stop to think of it, *secret confession* is a contradiction of terms. Secrecy is what makes confession necessary. And it is not surprising that the attempt to cope with unresolved personal guilt by means of continued furtiveness does not work out very well. Should we actually expect much to come of letting a priest, minister, psychiatrist, psychologist, social worker or some other "specialist" hear our sins if we continue to live the Big Lie with the people who really matter to us?
>
> As a result of my ongoing experience in group therapy, both in a mental hospital and in ordinary community settings, I am persuaded that healing and redemption depend much more upon what we say about ourselves *to others, significant others,* than upon what others (no matter how highly trained or untrained, ordained or unordained) say *to*

us. It's the truth we ourselves speak rather than the treatment we receive that heals us.[18]

As Joanna thinks about who the "significant" people are in her life, the obvious ones are her small group and her children away at college.

Let me sketch for you two little vignettes in her life during this period.

T*he Agony of Confrontation: Two Vignettes*

20
(Vignette One)

Joanna punched the Hartfords' big red pillow, recrossed her legs on the carpet, and pushed her back harder against the couch behind her. The group was finishing its study of "confession," and was about to move into "thanksgiving." Her heart was pounding. She knew what she had to do.

But Roger was concluding his remarks. "About this confession thing," he grinned. "I'm not trying to lay anything on *you* people, but I feel that *I* need to share with you what I struggle with, and as you pray for me and love me, God can break the back of my problem.

"I'm a 'Priority Two'[19] person. I'm so people-oriented, I spend all my spare time counseling, loving, teaching, going with people through their struggles, and on and on. I've really been tired lately. To tell you the truth, I think I've been tired for years! In the back of my mind, I know that the answer is 'Priority One,' that I need to relate more deeply to God. I have an *almost*-daily quiet time, mostly out of guilt, but I don't really long for him and linger with him and love to give him the quality time that would make me deeply rested. People wear us out, don't they? I need God first in my life.

"Will you guys please hold me accountable for a forty-five minute quiet time every day? That's my new measurable goal. Clare knows how I'm feeling spiritually drained. I love the Lord, but I've been living too much on my own resources, and I've come to a crisis point where he's calling me to make him truly 'Priority One' in my life."

Joanna perched on her cushion, spellbound. Roger was so wonderful; this couldn't possibly be a sin. She started to reassure him that he was great the way he was, but she felt the Holy Spirit check her. He had humbly expressed a need; inside herself, she knew he wanted to be taken seriously. It was she who broke the awkward silence.

"If the Lord will help me, Roger, I'd like to pray for you every day, that God will give you, that day, a really super forty-five minutes with himself."

Roger looked at her, and his eyes grew moist. He put his hand briefly over her hand and said, "Thank you, my sister."

The room seemed sweet, and full of love. Bruce said, "And I'll pray you'll get over feeling tired." The Body of Christ was functioning. Joanna felt encouraged, and with a rush she said,

"Roger, your confession compared to mine makes me feel like a Scarlet Woman! But the reason I ever came to this group was that the day before I came David had left me. He just walked out! I called Roger and Clare, and they invited me here."

She looked around at their faces, and knew that her news was truly a surprise. Somehow that made it harder to go on.

"Roger and Clare have been great in not spreading the story around, but *I've* got to tell it. Oh, don't think it was David's fault! I've been totally selfish and self-centered. He stood it as long as he could.

"But now that I've been starting to let God get to me, I feel maybe he'll make a new Joanna—and that David will come back, and we could start again."

The Agony of Confrontation: Vignette One

She ducked her head to hide her burning face, but the tears were flowing. "You all are really dear to me, and I'd sure appreciate it if you'd pray David will come back."

She couldn't say any more, and in an instant Susie was crouching beside her, hugging her and crying, too. "Oh, Joanna! Oh, you guys!" She looked around. "We're not doing all that great, ourselves! I hope Bruce doesn't mind my telling you, but we didn't go to Hawaii the way we said at all. We split—and he went to Las Vegas, and I went to my mom's. And things are still rocky...."

It was California earthquake time. The agendum for the meeting was forgotten, and for a long time tears, prayers, comfortings, and exhortations mingled together. One-upmanship had melted away; competition and surface talk were gone. The juices of the grapes had been pressured together into the wine of renewal, and eight Christian brothers and sisters drank deeply and felt refreshed and exhilarated as never before.

The meeting ended long after the usual time, as they stood in a circle with their arms around each other and sealed in prayer their promised commitment to each other for future mutual encouragement and prayer support.

Joanna blinked her eyes open once to take in the preciousness of the faces in that circle. The pressure of arms about her arms and back felt delicious—not in any way sensuous, as such pressures might have felt in former days, but pure and whole and right.

I feel totally nourished, she thought, with such love in my life. Thank you, Jesus.

21
(Vignette Two)

Joanna dug her bare brown legs into the warm beach sand, and hunted for Stevie's and Missie's familiar bodies somewhere out in the ocean's surf. She had called them home from college for the weekend, on the pretext that she was lonesome for them. But the moment they had burst into the house Stevie had crowed, "All right! Surf's up!" and they had dived into their swimwear, grabbed Steve's surfboard, and headed out the door.

Joanna was so anxious to be with them that she changed quickly into her suit, too, and drove down to their favorite surfing spot. Now, perched on a towel on the sand, she thought, this is going to be harder than telling Roger and Clare and the others. My goodness, I feel closer to my Christian brothers and sisters than I do to my own kids. Of course, she reflected, this hits a lot closer home. We're talking about their mother and father.

Instantly she felt made out of gelatin, and she prayed, Lord, thank you that six precious brothers and sisters are praying for me this Saturday afternoon, as I interact with my children at this very difficult level. I absolutely couldn't do it without their prayers.

What do people ever do without you, Lord? And what do Christians ever do without the support of a small group?

It seemed a long time before she saw them emerging from the water, tired and waterlogged. Steve was dragging his board; how strong his legs looked as they ploughed through the tide, she thought. Missie's wet body shocked her; her bra in no way covered her breasts, and her panties were not much more than a G-string. She noted that Steve's French cut was immodest, too, and she thought, my children have missed the influence of a truly Christian mother.

"Mom!" said Steve in surprise. "Hi!"

"I couldn't resist coming down," she said. "I have to see you all I can on a precious weekend like this. Have a seat, kids."

She threw them big beach towels; they wrapped up to their chins and sat down beside her. Steve's matted hair was black like hers, and when she looked at his face, at his high-arched nose and handsome cheekbones, she had the feeling of familiarity that she had when she looked in her own Baroque-framed mirror. Missie's wide-set eyes were steadfastly on her mother's as she tilted up a pretty, sandy-complected face, sprinkled through the wet with a few generous freckles. Each of the three waited, in tension, for the other to speak first.

"Stevie and Missie," began Joanna, "there doesn't seem to be any small talk, so let me just plunge right in." Dear God, telegraphed her heart! "I've got the most absolutely terrible news, and I have to share it with you, but please think with me that at least it must be just a temporary situation. . . ."

"If you mean about you and Dad," said Steve, "we know."

This possibility hadn't even occurred to her.

"You know?" she asked stupidly.

"We know," Steve said deliberately, and his voice sounded completely loveless.

"Daddy told us right away," volunteered Missie, with her big, questioning eyes. Suddenly the obvious query hung huge and unspoken between them—"Why didn't you tell us?" The silence seemed to make time stand still, until the crash of a wave on the beach in the background broke the spell.

"Stevie... *dear* Missie," she looked pleadingly from one face to another, "when your father left, I was thrown into a complete stupor. I was so embarrassed, I didn't want to tell anybody. I couldn't face the world. I couldn't—" She fished around for words, and finding none, began to cry weakly.

"I thought it would be patched up quickly, and you wouldn't ever have to know."

She was tempted to ask, "How did he tell you? *What* did he tell you?" but her emotions were too raw to endure the pain of learning details.

Still an awkward, pathetic poverty of expression hung between the three of them. If they knew when they first got home, Joanna wondered, why did they take off for the beach and ignore her? She supposed it was the embarrassment of being college-age kids not knowing how to cope with a difficult situation.

"Well, I gotta be going..." began Missie.

"No, no, *no!*" cried Joanna. "Listen! This is so important! I want you to know what's happening in my life! My goodness, you're my dear kids, and in a hard time like this, we've got to stay close...."

The two faces looked at her. "Okay, spill it," said Steve. "I have to admit, I sure wondered what was going on."

"It was all my fault." Joanna hastened to say. "Your daddy is a dear, and he's not to blame, but I was just selfishly doing my thing and not thinking what his needs were." She looked earnestly at them. "Oh, Stevie and Missie! Don't get married until you understand the sacrifice that true love requires!" (Pastor John's sermon was echoing in her heart.)

"Anyway, after this happened, I got into a group of Christians who meet once a week, and I've been listening hard to the pastor's sermons, and I've been reading my Bible, and God's been helping me begin to get my life squared away."

She dug her toes into the warm sand, and as she did, Missie changed position and her beach towel fell open. Joanna felt herself so distracted by that naked body that she felt strangely alienated from her children, as if her world were now so removed from theirs that there was no bridging the gulf. Questions flashed through her mind: were they sleeping around? Had they tried drugs? They had been raised so "carefully," according to the powerless standards of "churchianity"! She shot up another desperate telegram to the Lord.

"Has God been helping *you* two?" she asked. "What are you thinking? What are you feeling? Please tell me; I want to stay close to you."

"Well, Mom," said Steve, "you really did have it coming to you." (Pow! His effortlessly drawn gun fired straight into her heart.)

"Yeah," said Missie, "I mean, like, we could've walked out, too, but we were going off to college, so it didn't matter."

"You've never paid much attention to us. I mean, you were so busy having your clothes just—perfectly this and that, and running off to the beauty parlor all the time, and, you know, having in your darn groups—"

"Yeah," chimed in Missie. "Like, we never could sit on the white couches—"

"—I mean, like we felt we were in the *way* all the time. . . ."

Joanna was swallowing hard. And she had supposed they were so proud of their mother!

"It really doesn't matter, Mom," explained Steve. "We're grown and out of your hair, so I mean—what's the big deal, all right?"

"Wait! Wait a minute," cried Joanna. "You're my kids, and I love you! Why didn't you say any of this before?"

"You wouldn't have heard us," said Steve. "It's okay. Don't sweat it. I mean, on a scale of one to ten, you're not a *one*. Y'know what I mean?"

"Yeah, we love you, Mom," said Missie. "But, hey—I gotta

go. I promised Paula and Peter and the others that I'd come home one weekend soon anyway, so they'll start wondering if I don't check in, okay?"

Joanna tried to pull them back with words: "Kids, we really need to—to talk about this and get off to a fresh start—"

Steve and Missie had risen. "Yeah, Mom," said Steve. "For sure."

"Will you be home for dinner?"

"Uh, I don't think so," said Steve, and Missie shook her head.

"Kids, I really want you to go to church with me in the morning."

"Yeah, Mom," repeated Steve, already on his way. "For sure. . . ."

T Stands for Thanksgiving

22

Rain had been gently falling for hours in Corona del Mar. It had filled up Joanna's pool; it whispered against the windows. She sat curled on the couch in the den with her dinner tray over her lap. The television news was on, something about California mud slides. . . . She finished her dinner, laid aside the tray, and drew her knees up to her chin, feeling how delicious her peach satin at-home pajamas felt. She wasn't really eager to dress and go to the disciple group on such a night. But of course she rose to get ready.

For one thing, David seemed to have formed the habit of slipping in to do desk work on her group night, and it would be awkward to be here. Two fleeting thoughts: Would he come in the rain? And, David! I need you! David! Come back to stay!—But she was learning that grief eroded her disposition and accomplished nothing positive, so deliberately, she put him from her mind.

Lord, she said, there will be a special thrill in our all coming together on a night like this. It will show our commitment to each other. Oh, our fellowship in you is so sweet!

Besides, she thought, backing the Mercedes out of the garage and closing her garage door with the remote control button, I'm still totally dry and completely spoiled. . . .

Nevertheless, she was feeling like something of a martyr by the time she parked near the Hartfords' and tried to open her umbrella outside the car, gather up her notebook, Bible, and purse, and get out. Rain soaked her ankles, and she fell against the car door and pushed it shut with her raincoat in it. By the time she struggled to the front door, Roger was there to open it for her.

"Come in, come in!" he cried. "Look—the irony of it all—now that you're in, the rain is letting up."

"Oh, Roger," she exclaimed. "Shall I go back to the car and walk in again? Oh, I smell cocoa! How perfect!"

Joanna noticed that she was the first arrival. Her heart was warm with anticipation. How dear they all were—Roger and Clare, Susie and Bruce, Fred, Joyce, Marie! She strolled into the familiar master bedroom as if it were her own, and propped her open umbrella and raincoat in the big tub in the master bath, where they could drip.

Clare had filled a big silver bowl with polished red apples and laid cheeses on a pretty tray. "If I put out marshmallows for the cocoa, will you promise not to make one comment about calories?" she asked Joanna.

"Not a word, not a word," Joanna promised.

Roger and Clare and Joanna knelt on a couch in the den and looked out the big window behind it at the rain. A little waterfall streamed off the corner of the roof eave and was puddling below in an aster bed. They watched a neighbor darting out for a plastic-covered evening paper on his lawn, and then back to his house. . . .

Soon Joyce appeared and joined them on the couch; she had let herself in unannounced. "Move over, you guys," she giggled. "What's the passing parade? I'm embarrassed to be twenty minutes late; did you finish all the food?"

Suddenly they realized Susie and Bruce, Fred, and Marie were missing, and it was ten minutes to eight.

"Well, let's get on with the munchies," said Roger, "and maybe they'll walk in late."

So the four of them helped themselves to suddenly ridiculously large supplies of refreshments and, when the others had not arrived, settled down on the den floor in front of the fire; it was getting to be the custom.

Joanna was feeling hurt and disappointed. Where was Susie? The Bubble Machine had always had plenty of words; where were her actions to back them up? And Fred, still smarting because his wife had walked out on him, was always big on commitment. . . . She felt the Holy Spirit rebuking her quickness to hostility. How her two natures fought within her!

"I was going to kick off tonight by sort of reviewing a sermon on thanksgiving I got in the mail this week," said Roger, "since we're starting to study that. I just hate to do it when only half of us are here."

"All the important ones are present," volunteered Joyce. "Let's go."

"Read it to us, and put it in the mail for the others," suggested Joanna.

"I guess so," hesitated Roger. "Although the point of our coming together is sharing our reactions and sharing our lives and praying over what we're learning. They'll miss all that. If our times were purely informational and cerebral, I could just mail you the stuff every week and save your time." His disappointment was obvious.

"California Christians react to a little rain the way Canadians react to a blizzard," grumbled Clare. "I was with Marie not two hours ago."

"Anyway, here we go," said Roger. "This is a sermon by C. Parker Wright—I think he's called Chuck Wright—of the North Avenue Presbyterian Church in Atlanta. I get his sermons in the mail, and this one, called 'The Art of Giving Thanks,' fits right in. He says that 'ingratitude is the crisis of our time,' and that 'the cure for ingratitude is learning how to express praise and thanksgiving.' What d'ya think, is that about right?"

Nobody commented, so he went on.

"He says there are four steps to learning to be thankful. The first is having your focus on God rather than on material things or problems."

Roger stopped. "He's about to quote Romans 11:33-36, so we'd better turn to that, and somebody read it."

Clare read,

"Oh, the depth of the riches of the wisdom and knowledge of God!
   How unsearchable his judgments,
   and his paths beyond tracing out!
Who has known the mind of the Lord?
   Or who has been his counsellor?
Who has ever given to God,
   that God should repay him?
For from him and through him and to him are all things.
   To him be the glory forever! Amen."

Joanna said, "When I listen to that, I feel as if I'm standing at the far end of a giant throne room, and I know it's all fabulous, but I can't comprehend what I'm seeing. I wish we could just stop and spend the evening on those words."

"Well," said Roger, "gee whizz, that would be great; let's do it another time. But for now, let's just pick out the idea that everything has come from God. And as we live our lives praising God, the result will be that all things will move in a deep appreciation of him."

"Appreciation of God," mused Joanna out loud. "When you get disappointed in people, you can still appreciate God." An image of David flicked across her mental screen.

"In the earlier chapters of Romans, Paul's been talking about the Israelites' disobedience to God, and how they broke God's heart; and Paul had every right, humanly speaking, to be in despair.

"But he's like a mountain climber on a pinnacle! He can look back and see the eternity of God's goodness behind him. And he can look ahead and see God's marvelous plan to show his mercy to Israel, as he is to the Gentiles today, and that together everybody will praise him. And he just says, 'Oh, the riches! Oh, the glory of being where I am at this point in history!'

"Paul's only able to be thankful like that because his focus is on God. He's got perspective."

"Israel's life sounds like my life," said Joanna. "God picked me out a long time ago to be his own, but then I spent an awful lot of time fooling around, more or less unaware of him. . . . Am I talking too much?" She punched Joyce. "For goodness' sake, Joyce, say something."

"No, you're not," encouraged Roger. "And now, on a pinnacle, you can see that your eternity ahead is planned by God for his glory, and for your glory, too—and it's great, right?"

"Right," said Joanna. "Read on."

"Listen, my friend, God is in control of this universe. He is building his church around the world. Enjoy the sovereignty and power of God! Focus on him; center your praise on him.

"That's good, but, heck, I don't need to read it; I'll just tell you what he says," said Roger.

"First we focus on God. Step two, we recognize that there's a spirit of ingratitude in our natural hearts. And that spirit is really poisonous to our systems! It actually destroys creativity in God's people. It snuffs out artistic ability. It puts out the joy of living which ought to be inside us.

"Ingratitude is the heaviest sin of man." Roger stopped. "Anybody have a comment?" No comment.

"Our spirits can be released to be whole and happy and productive and positive when we're thankful. Gratitude is a powerful releaser and motivator for us. It's really important for us to know this!"

Roger's working up a head of steam, thought Joanna. She sneaked a look at her watch. I wish the others would come.

The group was looking at Deuteronomy 1, some shocking thing

about how if parents and elders of the Israelite community couldn't get a son who was rebellious and ungrateful to repent and change, even after much pleading, they were to stone him.

Roger was saying, "Why would God be so serious about the problem of ingratitude? Because he knows how destructive it is. It will snuff out a life, a marriage, a friendship, a family, a church, a business, a nation, a world, a universe! So God says, 'a son who absolutely insists on ingratitude and rebellion must die.' "

Joanna thought, Roger's really preaching tonight. We're all so dull, he has to carry the whole thing. What's the matter with us?

Roger was saying, "Any questions or comments?... Okay, review with me the way to thanksgiving. Step one, focus on God. Step two, recognize the poison of ingratitude. Step three, see that God has given a remedy in Christ.

"Now, step four: risk! Step out and express thank you's and praise, not only to God but to people around you...."

He broke off. "I feel like nobody's listening to me. This is good material, but it's a dumb evening."

"We're all owly because Susie and Bruce and Fred and Marie didn't come," volunteered Joyce.

"We thought we had such a great commitment," mourned Clare.

"I think," said Joanna, struggling to find the words, "after we had such a wonderful time last meeting, Satan's trying to shake us up, or break us apart—or something, I don't know what. But somehow, what we had was so good, and we mustn't lose it. What's happened?"

"Maybe we all caught my disease," offered Roger. "Our focus is on each other instead of on the Lord, so that when we're all functioning we feel great, and if we're not all functioning, we feel terrible. We must not lean most heavily on the second priority! Our emotions will go up and down like yo-yos. Just ask me; I know."

"Gosh," objected Joyce, "you gotta admit they're dirty rats, not to show up just because of a little rain."

"But, look," said Roger, "remember what we read in Romans 11?

'For from him are all things.' God allowed them not to come to teach us something. What is it?"

"To see that they're dirty rats?" offered Joyce.

"To look at God himself?" asked Joanna.

"I'm sure of it," Roger nodded. "Gee whizz, we've been reading that ingratitude is a poison that snuffs out the joy of living, that takes away our spirit—"

"—And we've been sitting here like *lumps,* with no joy of living, no spirit—" cried Joanna—

"—Because there's been no thanksgiving!" broke in Clare.

"Why don't we get on our knees," suggested Roger.

It was a special moment, a breakthrough into a new experience.

"Dear Father," began Clare, and she hesitated. Then—"You are just wonderful. You are perfect, and we stop right now to get our eyes back on you. Lord, we've been studying that adoration comes first, and we've gotten messed up when we so quickly forgot that. Forgive us.

"Father, we're so quickly swayed by every little circumstance! *I* am," she added. "I don't have to confess anybody else's sins. Forgive my being critical of Marie. Lord, she answers to you, not to me. All I have to do is love her, and I want to, right now. Please help me to be a more loving person."

After a silence, Roger began: "Lord, I want to thank you right now that you arranged this evening. You brought the four of us together. You wanted to teach us something that probably the others don't need to learn at all. They are very special people. Bless Susie and Bruce and Fred and Marie right now, wherever they are, whatever they're doing.

"We thank you for yourself. We thank you for them, and we thank you, we praise you that you are teaching us to give thanks in everything. Lord, don't let us be slow to learn.

"I pray for my own life, that I may put you first at all times, giving you the adoration of my heart, and quickly confessing to you every sin that comes up.

"And then, Lord (I know so little about it at this point), give me a mindset of thanksgiving, an ingrained habit of thanking you for everything that comes into my life. As Chuck said, it will keep my pipes cleaned out; it will keep the creative juices flowing—"

The telephone on the table shrieked so loud in the quiet that they all jumped.

"Gee whizz," said Roger, "from the sublime to the ridiculous. I forgot to take it off the hook. 'Scuse me. . . . Hello?"

In the silence that followed they heard Roger draw in his breath. "You're kidding!" he exclaimed.

Another silence. "She's all right, honest? . . . Bruce, are you at Hoag Hospital? . . . We'll be right there."

They were all wide-eyed. "The four of them were coming here together in Fred's car," said Roger, "and the wet streets were slick, you know, and they hit somebody, and I guess really banged up both cars. Susie got it the worst. They all went to Hoag Hospital; Bruce and Fred and Marie were treated and released, and Susie is there."

"Can we go?" asked Clare.

"It's too late for visitors," said Roger, "but the others are there. Let's go in my car."

The next few minutes were a nightmarish blur of city lights shimmering on black, wet streets, of cautious but furtive speeding, of anxious pauses at traffic lights. Along the way Roger prayed out loud at the wheel, "O Lord, protect Susie! Keep your everlasting arms underneath her; give the doctors wisdom; comfort Bruce and Fred and Marie. . . ." He prayed other things, with his three companions murmuring their amens but not hearing much. Out of the car—through the softly falling rain, with nobody noticing that they were getting wet—silently, hastily along the shining corridors—

"Roger!" called a soft voice from a door. They turned. "Come in, gang," whispered Bruce. "The nurse says it's okay for just a minute."

He led them into the room, around a white screen, and there in bed lay Susie. The side of her head was bandaged, and there was an unfamiliar look of strain and pallor on her face.

Joanna thought suddenly of "Bubble Machine," and contrition stabbed her heart. Lord, I'm sorry. . . .

"I'm really okay," Susie was smiling wanly.

Bruce went on to explain. "They checked her over a long time; that's why it was so late when I called you. And they say she's apparently just shaken up, with cuts and bruises. She has to stay here overnight for surveillance, but barring anything unforeseen, she's all right, and she can go home tomorrow."

"Dear Susie!" said Joanna. "We thank the Lord you're all right."

"I promised the nurse you'd just tiptoe in and out fast," and Bruce, "but I knew it would do her morale good to see you."

Roger took her hand briefly and prayed. The women bent over and gave her quick goodnight kisses: Fred touched her hand; and the group moved out and down the hall.

"How are *you* three?" asked Roger with concern.

"It was a miracle," said Bruce. "We're kinda shaky, but all we got were little cuts here and there from flying glass. Boy, you should've seen those two cars! There was only one person in the other car, and he's all right, too. It's just amazing."

"We'll take you all home," said Roger.

"Thanks, no," said Bruce. "The nurses are just going off their shift, and—you know how the Lord does—one of the nurses in emergency is Marie's neighbor, and she said she'd play taxi."

In a quiet corner by the exit door the group huddled with bowed heads, as Bruce offered a brief prayer. They found their hands were touching or clasping in holy oneness, and the presence of the Lord enveloped them in sweetness and power. Then, almost reluctantly, they moved to the door.

"We four had our own little crisis tonight, too," said Roger, quietly. "We'll tell you about it later."

S Stands for Supplication

23

Not a formula for prayer, but a lifestyle: ACTS.

A for adoration: recognizing God as God, and putting our eyes only on him, as we continually admire and worship him, as long as we breathe on this earth, and then into eternity.

C for confession: humbling ourselves to acknowledge that we need help, that we're not little gods somehow improving all the time, but that from God's perfect viewpoint we're worse than we know! And, having made that initial confession, then maintaining the habit of constantly confessing each new outcropping area of need.

T for thanksgiving: living in constant, happy gratitude for all his goodness to us, anyway. David the psalmist had it right. He prayed, "I'm not much, Lord"—and in his next breath—"but you've exalted me to top status!" (1 Chron. 17:16, 17, my paraphrase).

Adoration has a beginning time in our life when we want it to, by an act of our will. Then we're to make it our habit, our lifestyle.

Confession has a beginning time—tough, maybe traumatic, but essential. Confession to God and to all the right people. Then we're to make it our habit, too—and it isn't so hard any more.

Thanksgiving has a beginning time—for me, with the writing of this book! (I discovered that continual, happy gratitude was not an ingrained habit with me, and I confessed that, and he's helping me get started.) Then it also must become our constant way of life— thanking God for every circumstance as his perfect will, tailor-made for us, to enhance and perfect our exaltation. (Mysterious, amazing, wonderful!)

Adoration, confession, and thanksgiving, then, are the basis of our relationship with God. When we know him and live with him on those terms, we can live in continual renewal. And we can be audacious in asking him for things! Supplication naturally follows adoration, confession, and thanksgiving—and he is delighted for us to make huge requests.

And it's never because we deserve it, but because he loves us, and because he loves to give! And the more we ask and he answers, the more the cycle produces more adoration, confession, and thanksgiving on our part. What a happy way to live!

There is a high road to supplication which staggers the mind. God fills his Word with blank checks:

Ask and you will receive, and your joy will be complete (John 16:24).

This is the assurance that we have in approaching God: that if we ask anything according to his will, he hears us. And if we know that he hears us—whatever we ask—we know that we have what we asked of him (1 John 5:14, 15).

And James 4:2 says that we don't have because we haven't asked.

When George Mueller died, he left a notebook that contained fifty thousand specifically answered prayer requests in it. No wonder God used him!

The words *supplication* and *supply* are connected, and if any believer's life seems poorly supplied in any area at all, it could be because he hasn't really asked God.

There was a time in our first pastorate when we couldn't pay our coal bill. (We had a coal furnace in those days.) We felt bad about it—especially because we owed it to a member of the congregation and had to face him every Sunday! "Dear Lord," Ray and I prayed, "You really have to drop several hundred dollars down out of the blue, because we have no place to get this coal money."

So the Lord had the State of Iowa send us a letter. The State of Iowa has never written us before or since. But God gave Iowa a surplus in its budget right then, and he moved the lawmakers to decide to divide it among Iowa's veterans. And here came a letter of explanation and a check to Ray for the exact amount of the coal bill.

God loves for us to ask.

And God tells us in his Word how eager he is to answer our prayers. That's why he gave us the story of Daniel, for instance, who prayed—

—confessing his sin and trembling in weakness (see Dan. 9:20; 10:10)—

—and an angelic messenger appeared to reassure him like this:

"Daniel, you who are highly esteemed. . . . [because Daniel didn't say it, God could],

"Do not be afraid, Daniel. ["The fact that you tremble, Daniel, means that I will remove your fear."]

"Since the first day that you set your mind to gain understanding and to humble yourself before God, *your words were heard*" (Dan. 10:11, 12, emphasis mine).

Ray was preaching recently at University Presbyterian Church in Seattle. The time had come for prayer, and the choir began to sing an old hymn by John Newton that we almost never sing now, because the word *suit* had other meanings then than it does today. But the power of the message began to steal over me:

> Come, my soul, thy suit prepare;
> Jesus loves to answer prayer.

He himself has bid thee pray,
Therefore will not say thee nay.

The choir changed to a higher key. . . .

Thou art coming to a king:
Large petitions with thee bring;
For his grace and power are such,
None can ever ask too much!

24

Now, what if God decides to say no? Then we are entering into the fellowship of sharing in Christ's sufferings (Phil. 3:10). To the most important request of Christ's earthly life, his heavenly Father said no. As Christ faced the possibility of the cross, in almost unbearable anticipation "he fell with his face to the ground and prayed, 'My Father, if it is possible, may this cup be taken from me. Yet not as I will, but as you will'" (Matt. 26:29). Hebrews 5:7, 8 explains this further:

> During the days of Jesus' life on earth, he offered up prayers and petitions with loud cries and tears to the one who could save him from death, and he was heard because of his reverent submission. Although he was a son, he learned obedience from what he suffered.

Study this passage! It's not a lack of confidence in God that makes Christians pray for something and add, "if it's your will." (Sometimes that's disdained as showing a lack of faith, a way out.) Beware of "claiming" things from God, as if you knew better than he! God's Son was heard "because of his reverent submission." He made a strong request, but he added those words, "If it's your will, Father."

And "he was heard," but the Father in infinite wisdom said no.

And listen to what Christ said in Psalm 22, a Messianic Psalm prophesying his death a thousand years in advance: "My God, my God, why have you forsaken me?... O my God, I cry out by day, but *you do not answer*"!

A young pastor friend has in this last year been through the trial of his life. When I saw him recently, he asked me, "What do you do when God doesn't say yes—doesn't give it, doesn't make it happen?" Then he answered his own question: "Through agony I've gotten to know God better; I love him more...."

He showed me a piece of paper he keeps in his wallet. It says, "Look to his face, not to his hand."

But all this is not to say that God very often answers us with no! Be encouraged that he loves his children, and he loves to say yes! He can synchronize your heart with his, and empower you to ask the enormous things that delight him to answer—and delight you, too.

He opens himself up to you in Jeremiah 33:3: "Call unto me, and I will answer thee, and shew thee great and mighty things, which thou knowest not" (KJV).

And he offers you in Matthew 7:7,8 a powerful acrostic:

*A*sk and it will be given to you:
*S*eek and you will find;
*K*nock and the door will be opened to you.

And who but God himself can explain this dynamic, sweeping conclusion: "For everyone who asks receives; he who seeks finds; and to him who knocks, the door will be opened"?!

The question we have to ask ourselves is, *what is it we really want?*

If we want just an ordinary life, God will give us that. If we want to hang onto our personal sins at any cost, God honors the free will he gave us. We'll just miss all the fun and all the rewards.

There were a couple of fellows who had to make a sudden emergency trip across one of the Great Lakes of North America. They raced to the water's edge just as daylight was leaving, and found a boat there, and started rowing for all they were worth.

All night long they rowed. The winds lashed at them, the cold chilled their bodies, their arms ached with fatigue. But as morning began to dawn, they saw the shore in the distance. And they knew they were going to make it.

Then it got lighter—and they looked around to discover that the boat had a motor! In the dusk and in their haste they hadn't noticed it! If they'd known, they could have crossed the lake with perfect ease.

That's how it is with our lives, if we're members of God's family. We can struggle and worry and fret our way through life, and we'll still make heaven and make perfection, because God has promised our destination, either way. It will just be tough going until we get there.

Or we can discover the motor he's provided: the Holy Spirit's empowering us to be "ACTS" Christians!

We can adore him continually.

We can confess each sin instantly, and be instantly forgiven.

We can thank him for anything and everything.

And then we can ask and ask and ask! We can be really greedy!

25

Ray and I were flying when we read this paragraph in a flight magazine. It has lived with us ever since:

> Make no little plans. They have no magic to stir men's blood. . . .
> Make big plans. Aim high in hope and work. . . . Let your watchword
> be order, and your beacon, beauty.[20]

Let your mind expand! Believe that God will do large, wonderful things—and that he'll get all the credit. Call on his Holy Spirit to tell you what to ask for. Then your requests will be much bigger and more important and exciting than if you were on your own.

Don't be the kind of person who looks at the Lord through the wrong end of a telescope! Don't see him as small. He owns everything, and he has all power. He distributes the world's commodities and time and power to whomever he pleases. And this God asks us to ask him for things! He says, "If you remain in me and my words remain in you, ask whatever you wish, and it will be given you" (John 15:7).

Remaining or staying close in him, and letting his words sink deep into you—those are the magic keys.

Then here's what will happen. Just as a clay pot takes its shape from its mold, so will your will be formed in the mold of the will of God. Then you will have everything your own way!

It's the old saying, "Love God, and do as you please." Because when you perfectly love him, *you will please what he pleases*.

It will be the most fun, most wonderful life possible. Daily you'll be "adoring" him, admiring him. When you "goof," you'll admit it and get it taken care of immediately. You'll let your heart bubble up in continual thanks for everything—everything. And you can ask and ask, because your will will be "in sync" with his.

Last year Ray was preaching to all the U.S. Army Protestant Chaplains stationed in Europe; they were gathered in Berchtesgaden, West Germany, for their annual retreat. Here are some of the notes I took on one of his messages:

> Ephesians 3:20, 21: "Now to him who is able to do immeasurably more than all we ask or imagine, according to his power that is at work within us, to him be glory in the church and in Christ Jesus throughout all generations, for ever and ever! Amen."
>
> Don't think it's immature to ask things of God. Don't scoff at the "gimmies." God says he's able to do for us immeasurably more. . . . Ask hugely!
>
> What should we ask for? When God gives fullness of Spirit, young men dream dreams, old men see visions. The more we're filled with him, the larger and bolder our prayers can be; the bigger will be our view of God.
>
> We ask little because we think little, and we think little because we see a little God. Stretch your vision to see who he is, and your requests of him will stretch and stretch.
>
> And they won't be to glorify you. When you are in the Spirit, your requests will glorify God. The Holy Spirit is wholesome, not bizarre. We will not strut. We will pray largely for important things.
>
> Result: "glory," verse 21. The splendor of God—in two places: in the church and in Christ.

"All God's great people have been ordinary people who counted on God's being with them in power."

A mother once took her little boy to hear Paderewski, the great pianist. At the beginning there was simply a bare stage with a spotlight focused on the grand piano and bench. The mother and son had come half an hour early, and eventually the little boy got restless. Somehow, the mother got absorbed in reading the program, and when she finally looked up, his seat was empty! She looked everywhere around her, and he was nowhere to be seen.

Then—her heart was in her throat—suddenly she heard the sound of "Chopsticks." There he was on stage, in the spotlight, picking away on the long concert grand!

"Get him out of there!" came voices from the crowd.

"No!" cried a European accent from the wings, and the great Paderewski strode on stage. "Boy, keep going. I'll help you."

And he sat down on the bench next to the little fellow and began adding fabulous improvisations—chords, patterns, runs, and additional melodies—as the two of them entranced the packed house with "Variations on Chopsticks"!

> In the same way, the Spirit helps us in our weakness. We do not know what we ought to pray, but the Spirit himself intercedes for us with groans that words cannot express. And he who searches our hearts knows the mind of the Spirit, because the Spirit intercedes for the saints in accordance with God's will (Rom. 8:26, 27).

When we pick at our pathetic little prayers, suddenly we are not alone. Someone has come alongside us, and we have moved into a duet of greatness beyond our dreams.

26

And now, who is ready to enter into this New and everlasting Covenant with his whole heart? Let each of us do it.

Begin by asking God very humbly to give you, by the Spirit who dwells in you, the vision of the heavenly life of wholehearted love and obedience, as it has actually been prepared for you in Christ. It is an existing reality, a spiritual endowment out of the life of God which can come upon you. . . . Ask earnestly, definitely, believingly, that God reveal this to you. Rest not till you know fully what your Father means you to be, and has provided for your most certainly being.

"When you begin to see [it], . . . offer yourself to God unreservedly to be taken up into it.[21]

Renewal Has a Fruitbearing Time

27

"God!" cried Joanna, driving home from shopping, as she slipped her Mercedes into the garage. "The pain doesn't get less, it gets more! There's no Fiat in the other parking space. There's no atmosphere of David's presence in this big, empty house. There's no—" she hesitated, and then poured it all out to her merciful and understanding Father: "There's no satisfying of my physical needs, Lord," she said. She slumped over the steering wheel and wiped a tear.

"And more, there's no psychological satisfaction—no challenge to my spirit to satisfy a husband—to meet his needs, to make him happy, to live for him. I had no vision to do that, Lord, for so many years. But now I do, and it makes the agony of his absence even more intense. Father, I long to try again! Lord God, I miss him dreadfully! I'm incomplete! I hurt! O God, I hurt!" Sobs shook her shoulders.

The telephone was ringing. Lord, said Joanna inwardly, as she grabbed her grocery bag and slipped out of the car, you just don't want me to indulge in self-pity, do you!

She set the bag on the kitchen counter. Still, Father, I need a good cry sometimes, and it seems as if you cut that one a little short; it's still in my system.

It helped a great deal to tell him everything she was thinking and feeling. "Hello."

It was Clare. "Joanna, Pastor John is calling a special time of prayer this evening for anyone interested. Do you have plans?"

"I was going out to dinner with Joyce," said Joanna. "Actually, that doesn't need to take all evening. What time are you meeting? And could Joyce come, too?"

"At seven thirty. And of course. Actually, I was phoning everyone in our group, so you're saving me a call."

"I'll ask her. She'll say yes. We'll be there," said Joanna.

Joanna and Joyce headed for one of Newport Beach's favorite restaurants, sure that they'd come early enough to avoid waiting. But the entryway was already crowded, and they got in line. A dozen or so people ahead of them waited their turn at the dining room door. Surely, thought Joanna, surveying the crowd ahead of her, this area is full of "the beautiful people"—at least as far as the world judges beauty.

Then she froze, fascinated. There was David's handsome profile ahead of her in line, and he was looking down and smiling at a chic little number at his side. Joanna hoped Joyce wasn't aware that she was staring. He needs a haircut, she thought. It's over his collar just the tiniest bit. . . . Oh, that beautiful head. . . .

The girl at his side said something. He threw back his head and laughed. Then he reached around her tiny waist and gave her a quick hug, and his big, familiar hand reached further down and gave her bottom a pinch. . . .

"Joyce," said Joanna faintly, "we'll never get to church at seven thirty if we wait in this line."

"You're right," said Joyce. "I hated to mention it because the food's so good, but you're right."

"Let's go ... somewhere else. ..." Joanna was stumbling out. "Anywhere. ..."

*   *   *

It was a blank hour and a half later.

"Joanna," Pastor John was saying, "thanks so much for coming." His voice, so familiar in the pulpit, seemed somehow unexpectedly close, and Joanna felt shy.

"Well, I need it," she answered. "Not it—*Him*. Thanks for letting me be included in a prayer time."

People were crowding the door behind them, and Pastor John raised his voice to address perhaps thirty-five or forty people.

"Wow, you all are *great*. I hoped for a dozen or fifteen people, but I guess the word spread. Boy, this really encourages me."

Then he said, "Folks, I need you to join me in special prayer tonight for our church, and I'd like it if we prayed right in the front rows of the sanctuary, right where we long to see the action happen. Are you all up for that?"

There was a murmur of consent, and they moved down the center aisle and filled in the first pews.

Pastor John was repeating, "Friends, I'm excited! I'm encouraged that you're concerned about our church as I am, and the most obvious thing for us to do is to pray.

"So I don't want to take much time with introductory remarks; we need to get right on with it. But let me just briefly share a couple of thoughts from Myron Augsburger's book, *Called to Maturity*. [22]

"The first page is a prayer, which ends with these words:

> We long to drink deeply from the satisfying stream of thy love,
> To know and be filled with thy presence and thy glory.

"I feel you people are with me in sharing that longing. We're all somewhat frustrated, going through the right motions every Sunday here in this very room, but not sensing that we're filled with his presence and his glory.

"I've been studying the formula A-C-T-S lately (that's adoration, confession, thanksgiving, and supplication), searching for a basis on which we can all ask God strongly for spiritual renewal in this church. And I'm seeing more and more that this three-legged stool is a good, sturdy one on which to plant ourselves.

"We must give ourselves earnestly to the adoration of God—together as a people in this sanctuary, with all the excellence and care we can muster.[23] And we must adore him continually in our individual hearts. It's our first and highest business. No less than God himself can be 'Priority One' in our lives.

"This exalted view of God among us will keep us in a spirit of humility before him. I see that we must be forever sensitive to our own sins, and quick to confess them the instant his Spirit puts a finger on them. I long to live before you in openness and vulnerability, confessing my sins as he prompts me to. Boy, I've got plenty, and the Lord has to help me in this.

"And then I see that, as a church and individually, we must live in a spirit of thanksgiving. Otherwise, when we get aware of God, and aware of our own sins, we'll wonder what's the matter with all the rest of the morons around us who aren't so aware, and we'll get critical and fussy. I confess to you right now, I get so impatient for renewal and fresh reality in this church, my heart often fusses over it! And that grieves the Lord. He wants me to follow Philippians 4:6,7; listen to this:

> Do not be anxious about anything, but in everything by prayer and petition, with thanksgiving, present your requests to God. And the peace of God, which transcends all understanding, will guard your hearts and minds in Christ Jesus.

"So our strong petitions to God can't be offered with a fussing, critical attitude. We have to love our dear people *just as they are,* the way God loves them, and fill our hearts with thanksgiving for everything positive, as a prerequisite to our supplications."

He grinned and looked around. "What do you think? Does that sound right?"

"Amen," murmured several.

"Augsburger's got some great sentences in his little book. Like, 'Revival is the "Reviver" at work.' That's good, isn't it! Let's ask God to work deeply on all of us.

"And, speaking of revival again, he says, 'There is a need in every generation for such a spiritual renewal.' I believe that. Newport Beach hasn't seen revival within my memory. It's time. We can't live on the spiritual experiences of a generation ago.

"Again, he says,

Revival is a spiritual renewal in realigning your life with the Word and will of God. This is more than conviction; it's correction. It is not enough to recognize our imperfections; we must renounce them. The great problem with the church is not that we have poor doctrines, but we are poor in living them.[24]

Oh, yes, cried Joanna's heart.

"Friends, don't pray for renewal unless you are willing for changes in lifestyle."

Soon it was time for prayer. After a silence, Pastor John began:

"Lord, I'm excited over you. You must have plans for us, to call all these dear people together like this. God, there is no God like you! We look up into your face, and we say, 'Alleluia. You are so wonderful. Wherever you're going, that's where we want to go, too.... '" Pastor John paused, and then went on with difficulty.

"Lord, I don't know how I can be some Big Deal to lead these precious people when I look at my own weaknesses and sins. Father, I need to confess to you in front of these my friends, who will love me and not be too hard on me, that I felt you prodding me to call them together to pray months ago, but I'm just plain shy. I have the courage of a lion, preaching in front of the whole congregation. But one on one, I get intimidated by people.

"You know that my concern for renewal has been genuine, Father. But it's easier for me to pour my heart into sermon preparation, and think I'm being an adequate pastor behind closed doors, than to mingle with these dear people face to face."

(With a shock, Joanna realized there was some truth here; she had only been close to him in quick handshakes at the door after services. Then she wondered fleetingly if Roger's loving aggressiveness might have instigated Pastor John's small group of men.)

"In other words, Father," he was continuing, "my preoccupation with myself has really hindered the spiritual progress of this church. Lord, I'm sorry! Lord, I confess this as a great sin. Lord, I'm sorry—!

"But I do believe in the sovereignty of God, and that you make good come out of all things, and I have to believe that your timing is right. Maybe all of us together wouldn't have been ready until now. Thank you, Lord, that your love so magnificently overrules, and that, in spite of us, you are carrying out your plans.

"And so, Lord, we are bold to ask you a huge thing. O Lord, send revival to this church! Lord, do such a public thing among us that all Orange County will know it, marvel, and be affected by it! O Lord, please! Show us your glory! O Father, may Jesus Christ become the most talked-about Person in Newport Beach!"

Other prayers followed. The people prayed for illnesses of friends and relatives; they prayed for their country and for their governmental leaders; they thanked the Lord for many blessings; they prayed for the church's missionaries around the world. . . .

After most of an hour, Roger stood to his feet. Joanna thought she had never seen him look so shaken.

"Friends," he said quietly, but his voice cracked, giving away his emotion, "our pastor has asked us to pray for revival, and we're going all around Robin Hood's barn! Forgive me for being agitated; prayer is wonderful, of course—any prayer. But, by cracky—" (the expression's very corniness somehow revealed Roger's passion) "I think we left our courage at home tonight."

He looked around the group. "What are we afraid of? Does revival threaten us? Do we fear it would touch our wallets, or alter our lifestyles a little? Do we fear change? Do we fear the unfamiliar? Are we so unused to being totally sold out to Jesus Christ that we'd rather just ask him to heal Aunt Martha's big toe?" The silence was deafening. "I think the subjects of our prayers have been inappropriate tonight.

"Sure, I'm kinda scared, too," he went on, "but Pastor John said we could expect renewal or judgment—one of the two—and I think I'm more scared of judgment."

He paused, awkwardly. "Well, I'd like to pray, now." And beside his pew he dropped to his knees!

" 'Lord, be merciful to me, a sinner,' " prayed Roger. "I don't know what to say. . . . I've been spouting off, but it's not that I'm any *better* than anyone here. O Lord, look upon us in mercy. Forgive my sounding judgmental.—Boy, Lord, I don't dare, the way I snapped at Clare at the dinner table tonight."

He stopped. "Clare, will you forgive me?"

There was a silence, and Clare must have nodded, because Roger resumed his prayer. "Lord, make me a loving, patient husband. Wash me—and bring revival—to me, to us, and to our church."

Joanna felt a kind of groaning in her soul, over whether or not people would respond. Did renewal always demand birthpangs, she wondered?

There was a long, heavy silence. Feet shifted. Throats cleared. Joanna asked, Lord, do you want me to pray first? It seems as if there are so many important people here, who are at the heart of the church, and I'm on the fringe, and a novice in all this. . . . She felt agitated over the silence, and disappointed that nothing significant was happening.

At long last one of the fellows spoke up. "Thank you, God, for

Roger's rebuke. He's dead right. I, for one, love the pastor, and I was glad to come pray for our church, but I didn't know you were going to poke your finger right into my heart and start prying around. Lord, uh, here I am, and I ask you to cleanse me and start me fresh with you."

Another long silence. It seemed almost unbearable to Joanna. Father, she prayed, we don't need dozens praying at once, we just need one at a time. Just one, now, Father, please just one, for each moment as needed, who'll have the courage to pray with his mask off.

The Holy Spirit seemed strongly prompting her to be the one! "Dear Father in heaven," began Joanna out loud, "you've just been becoming real to me lately, through my troubles—through my husband David's and my separation. Lord, I'm sorry it took so long for you to get through to me. I must have been a real pain to you for so many years. I was so self-centered!"

Joanna stopped for a moment, praying about what she should say next. "Lord, spiritual renewal is fantastic! I know, because you've been bringing renewal lately to my life, and to the small group I'm in, too. It's the greatest thing I could wish for our church.

"So, Father, I'd like to ask you for two things. Please bring revival to our whole church, and—please bring David back to me." There! It was out. Her voice had quivered a little, but she'd said it, and she was excited about it.

Lord, she went on silently, I'm learning to adore you, and I'm learning to confess my sins, and I want to learn to be thankful more and more—so haven't I met the qualifications? Won't you please answer my 'supplication,' and 'supply' me with a husband?

In her concentration she hardly realized at first that others were praying, quite steadily now, and there seemed a quiet reality and openness to their prayers. You're doing it, Father, she rejoiced! You're already answering what I asked: one at a time, with their masks off!

Many prayed for the church, and many prayed for themselves, too.

A man prayed, "Father, you know how I've rebelled over this cancer of mine; I've fought it so angrily, I've made all my family around me miserable. Lord, tonight I surrender to you. You love me, Lord, and maybe you've got great plans in this cancer that I wasn't willing to see. I submit totally now to your will for my life, and I pray I'll be a blessing to my family, not a curse." (There were sounds, here and there, of sniffing and noses blowing.)

Joanna thought about that. Then she told the Lord silently, Well, Father, I still think you'll bring David back, but I vow right now that I'll praise and thank you, either way.

At one point a man stood and prayed with great, unusual fervor for God's Holy Spirit to bring his wind of cleansing and freshness and renewal to the church. He quoted much Scripture as he prayed, repeating God's own promises for renewal back to God. Joanna sensed a particular authenticity of the Spirit in his prayer, and sensed over all the people a lifting and relief and hope. Remembering what Roger had been teaching their small group about supplication, she had a thought that this evening's prayers could become a crowbar, a powerful lever to lift their entire congregation out of apathy and lethargy.

Later a woman prayed, "God, this time together is so sweet, surely it can't be the end. How do we carry on from here? Lord, give wisdom to Pastor John as he leads us."

With that, the pastor concluded the prayer time, and then stood at the front and looked at all of them.

"This has been a holy time, hasn't it?" and there was a quiet shining on his face.

"Francie's right, of course, and I've been praying about what should happen next. I haven't checked it out with the Board, but several of them are here tonight. Gentlemen, if I can be so informal and unofficial, would you think it appropriate for us to meet here again Sunday night, and just wait on the Lord, and continue whatever he wants to do among us?"

Heads were nodding vigorously. One of the elders spoke up: "I was thinking exactly the same thing. Pastor, let me phone around to the other Board members to make it official, but I know it will be fine."

Going down the church steps. Joanna remembered David with that girl in the restaurant. Lord, what a remarkable evening. . . . My heart has far more peace about David now. How this meeting has comforted and nourished me!

That night she slept very well.

28

Joanna came fifteen minutes early on Sunday night, out of sheer excitement. But already the parking lot was starting to fill up, and as she walked from her car through the late-afternoon sunshine, she squeezed hands or gave quick hugs to many brothers and sisters she knew.

Good grief! she gasped, as she walked into the sanctuary. The place was getting full of people! She slipped into a pew. Father! You are too much! She flipped pages in her Bible at random, and her eyes settled on 2 Chronicles 20:12,13:

> O our God, . . . we have no power to face this vast army that is attacking us. We do not know what to do, but our eyes are upon you.
> All the men of Judah, with their wives and children and little ones, stood there before the Lord.

My, thought Joanna, this must be battle time for us, too. Satan surely must be nervous when God's people start getting excited over him! I wonder what is happening in and around this sanctuary, if I had eyes to see! Lord, keep me in vigilant prayer.

Still, people kept filling up the pews, and by the time Pastor John rose to speak, the sanctuary was full.

"Dear people," he said. "let's pray." At once they were on their knees! It happened without suggestion. It was as if hundreds of people could hardly wait to fall down before the Lord.

There was a silence, pregnant with earnestness. Then from here and there over the sanctuary young and old, men and women began offering prayers.

"Lord, I've really goofed this term in not studying. I mean, I really deserve my lousy grades. Please give me the discipline to really concentrate, for you. Y'know—my parents have poured so much money into sending me to college. Lord, I'm really sorry! Please forgive me, and really start me fresh, so I can encourage them, too. . . ."

"God, you're wonderful! I sure do love you."

"O Lord, my big mouth gets me into so much trouble! Please help me to be a gentle, loving wife and mother. . . ."

"Lord, I've been so critical of that Trustee Board this term! Having been a Trustee before, I thought I knew it all. Forgive my tongue and my critical spirit. Father, those Trustees are magnificent men, with a hard job to do. Bless Harry, Stan, George, Bob, Ivan, and Vic." Noses were blowing.

A very old man, much revered in the church, quavered,

> "Through many dangers, toils, and snares,
>   I have already come;
> 'Tis grace hath brought me safe thus far,
>   And grace will lead me home."

And everybody spontaneously clapped for him! This sweetness is almost too much to bear, thought Joanna.

"Lord, I pray that what's happening here tonight will spread to all of Orange County and throughout Southern California. . . ."

"Father, I surely love all these brothers and sisters here. . . ."

Someone broke into singing, and everyone joined in:

Turn your eyes upon Jesus,
  Look full in His wonderful face;
  And the things of earth will grow strangely dim
    In the light of His glory and grace.[25]

"Lord, how I pray for our pastor! Thank you for the touching way he opened up his heart to us Thursday night. Father, give him a happy new liberty with people on a one-to-one basis. Thank you for him."

One-to-one basis. The personal-relationship-thing sent into Joanna's mind a sudden thought of Betsy. She hadn't had contact with her since that awful phone conversation over the tennis date. Joanna peeked to make sure she had a quarter. Then, clutching her purse and murmuring to be excused, she slipped out of the pew and disappeared for a little to make an apologetic phone call. Eventually she was back, wearing a look of relief and joy. Who could know that she also had had a request from Betsy to join her in church next Sunday?

A woman was praying, "Lord, I've just been involved in this church because of my husband, and I knew people were praying for my salvation, particularly Andy and Julie, and it embarrassed me and made me defensive. Lord, forgive me! Jesus Christ, I do now ask you to come into my life and be my Savior." ("Whooppee!" called out a young guy's voice, and everyone broke into laughter.)

"God, I've been so bugged over my roommate" (the girl praying stopped to sniffle), "but tonight you've given me a new love for her. Please help me to be able to tell her so right away."

From somewhere else in the sanctuary a young girl got up, made her way to this one, and the two of them fell into each others' arms, crying!

"O Lord, until recently that's the way it was with our marriage." It was Bruce's voice. "Susie and I want to thank you together for the great new love you've given us for each other."

"Oh, yes, Lord!" added Susie, "it's so wonderful! And Bruce is so wonderful! And Pastor John's so wonderful! And the church is so wonderful! And you're so wonderful!" Joanna thought the bubbles had never sounded so good.

Then there was a cry of agony: "O God, we want that kind of marriage, too. Please help us."

And another voice, "So do we, Lord."

From the front row, one of the young men: "Lord, you love me so much!"

And from a back row, all the way to the front, another young man's voice: "And I love you, too, Joe!" Again, sanctified laughter!

Amazing! Marvelous! Joanna's heart was skipping and leaping on high places. Already she knew what she must pray:

"Father, I've never tithed before, but suddenly I know that I not only need to give you lots more than a tenth, but I've got so much to make up from the past. In this Newport Beach area where the prices are high, there must be plenty of brothers and sisters hurting, and others as well. You've opened up my heart; now open up my purse."

... Many hours later, Joanna sensed restlessness and much shifting of positions in the quiet. For the first time she was more aware of her knees than of the circumstances! Apparently others were, too, because one of the young fellows began to sing, "Stand up, stand up for Jesus—" and the people burst into delighted laughter, joining in the singing as they rose to their feet.

There was general stretching and a hubbub of happy relief over the crowd, and everybody knew that the Lord had ended the evening. From the front Pastor John grinned, "Good night."

Joanna gave lots of hugs on the way out to both men and women, and touched cheeks with her kisses. She noticed many of the men with their arms around each other, too. There was lots of laughing, and a bunch sang "Happy birthday, dear Ruthie" to the wife who'd become a Christian. In little knots here and there over the room, twos and threes still had their heads together in prayer. And in one spot Joanna noticed two business tycoons, who'd had a feud going in their Newport Beach businesses for years, hugging. . . .

Moonlight flooded the parking lot. In high mood Joanna playfully patted her Mercedes. "You poor thing," she sympathized, "you're only a car, and you have no soul or spirit in you to feel what human beings can feel—I mean, people who get in touch with God."

Then her eyes grew thoughtful. "Anne."

Anne: "Who, me?"

Joanna: "If you can interrupt me, can't I interrupt you?"

Anne: "Well, I don't know. Golly, you startled me."

Joanna: "I want to apologize for how I acted to you. And thank you for making me stick it out."

Anne: "Thank you for saying so, dear. . . . What wonderful days these are for your church!

"Incidentally, I can't resist telling you: every single incident and comment in your meeting times Ray and I have witnessed and heard, when we've been with groups experiencing God's reviving and renewing."

Joanna: "Are you serious? Words fail me."

Anne: "Exactly! Me, too! That's my problem with this book!"

Joanna: "God is so wonderful."

Anne: "Yes. And I love you, Joanna. I really do."

29

"Joanna," chirped a young girl's voice over the phone, "you don't know me, but I'm Cheryl, Fred's daughter—you know, in your group—and three of my girlfriends and I really need you to disciple us. Could we please get together with you? I mean, do you have time?"

"Oh, my goodness," said Joanna, "I don't know very much! I'm just getting going, myself."

"Hey, you know a bunch," chided Cheryl. "You've been in my dad's groups for months, now. How 'bout all that good stuff? Just pass it on to us girls, okay?"

"Are you serious? Do you really want me?" Joanna felt excited to think that maybe this was why she had also just joined a women's Bible class.

"Listen, Joanna," said the serious young voice. "We not only want you, we need you, all right? Can you believe, only one of the four of us gals has a *mother*? We really need a substitute mother in Christ—okay?—to love us and help us really move in closer to God. . . ."

"You're on," said Joanna.

* * *

"Marie!" exclaimed Joanna, nearly bumping into her friend in the aisle of a store. "I didn't see you behind all those packages. Are you buying out the whole place?"

"I'm buying for the next two years!" gasped Marie. "Oh, Joanna, I found out that a school for missionary kids in Nigeria needs a dorm mother, and they asked me, and I'm going!"

"Hey, wait a minute," cried Joanna. "I've been with you every week, and you never said a thing. . . ."

"Well, my cousin is the principal, and a dorm mother got sick so there was this sudden vacancy, and he knows me so well, he didn't have to check me out, he just *asked.* And I said *yes!*" Her eyes were excited.

Joanna just stood there. "You, Marie—a missionary—?"

"Hey, come on," said Marie. "it's not that funny—"

"No, it's wonderful," said Joanna. "But slow down on the buying. The group's got to give you a shower. And good night, we've got to figure out your support. We never had a real live missionary to take care of before!"

* * *

Joanna took a child's hand firmly in each of hers. "Come on, Melinda; come on, Janie," she said cheerily. "You're going to love your new school. It's really nice here."

Melinda looked apprehensive as they entered the big building. "Where do you go the the bathroom?" she asked in a small, anxious voice.

"Let's find out even before we go see your teacher," said Joanna. The three of them went down the big, pale green hall.

"Let's see, here it says 'girls' on the door. All right? You go right in there." She looked down at Melinda. "Okay?"

Melinda's eyes were filling with tears.

"Do you want to go now?" asked Joanna. Melinda nodded.

"Sure, no problem. Let's see, in we go. Here are lots of nice little rooms. Let's go in this one. Shall I help you with your panties? You can do it yourself? Great. Janie and I will wait right outside the door for you."

Soon Melinda emerged, and offered a wan smile.

"Janie, would you like to go, too? No? Okay, would you like to go see your nice new teachers now? Let's go find out where you go."

Into the attendance office. Forms to fill out. Then an explanation to the principal, behind closed doors: "Mrs. Jackson, their father came out to California from Indiana thinking he had a job, which didn't materialize, and they're hurting financially. Our church found out about it, and we're just pitching in to care for them until they can get on their feet. All right? If you have any questions, let me give you my name and number to call first, because their mother is sick right now. I'll be back at two thirty to pick them up."

Lord, said Joannā, on the way out of the school door, there's never a dull moment with you.

* * *

The doorbell was ringing. Susie must be here to take me to the prayer service.

Joanna skipped down the big staircase. "I'm coming!" she sang out as the bell rang again. "Watch out, Lady Magdalene, I don't want to fall over you."

She was memorizing a verse, and she repeated it on the way to the door: "Psalm 107:9. 'For he satisfies the thirsty and fills the hungry with good things.'"

She opened the door. It wasn't Susie; Joanna could see Susie beyond, waiting at the curb in her car. This was a messenger, standing there in the sunshine, and he handed her an envelope.

"Thank you!" she smiled brilliantly, and tossed back her black hair as she opened it.

It was divorce papers. . . .

The sunshine seemed to grey down, darker and darker. How cold were the black letters on those cruel white pages! David? My David, sweet, big, predictable, freckled. . . . David, are *you* behind this ugly thing? The floor seemed to reach up for her, to suck her heart out of her body, the senses out of her life.

Still she stood. Time no longer seemed to matter. . . . Except that time was urgently trying to reenter her consciousness again: Susie's steps were trotting toward her on the sidewalk.

"Joanna? Is something wrong?"

Wordlessly, Joanna offered her the documents. Susie looked, frowned, gasped with comprehension, dropped the papers to the floor, and stood with hands spread open before Joanna, as if simply to offer whatever she could, whatever she had. . . .

Joanna accepted. She put her trembling body next to Susie's, and Susie wrapped her around with love. The Bubble Machine was turned off. The two women stood so, one silently praying strength into the other, for a long time. Then they went out the door, and into the car.

It seemed to turn churchward purely from habit, winding past charming houses on streets that followed curves—the curves of those softly rounded hills that are Corona del Mar.

Overhead, sea gulls wheeled, squealing their cries.

Against the nearby rocky coast, white waves foamed endlessly, endlessly.

And above them, one small plane lazily dipped and buzzed.

Notes

1. Ray Ortlund and Anne Ortlund, *The Best Half of Life* (Waco, Tex.: Word Books, 1976), p. 15.
2. Psalm 102:26, 27.
3. See Raymond C. Ortlund's *Lord, Make My Life a Miracle* (Glendale, Calif.: Regal Press, 1974).
4. A. W. Tozer, *The Knowledge of the Holy* (New York: Harper & Row Pubs., 1978), p. 6.
5. Quoted in the Pasadena, Calif. *Star-News,* 24 July 1978.
6. Ibid.
7. Ibid.
8. Adapted from Lewis Sperry Chafer, *Grace* (Chicago: Moody Press, 1947), pp. 308–310.
9. Thomas Howard, "Who Am I? Who Am I?" *Christianity Today,* 8 July 1977, pp. 12, 13.
10. Charles Hadden Spurgeon, *The Treasury of the New Testament,* vol. 3 (Grand Rapids, Mich.: Zondervan Publishing House, 1950), p. 417.
11. Song of Solomon 7:8–12.
12. William Cowper, 1731–1800.
13. Ernest Dimnet, *The Act of Thinking* (Greenwich, Conn.: Fawcett Publications, reprinted by Simon and Schuster, 1928), pp. 120, 121.
14. Nicholaus L. von Zinzendorf, 1700–1760; tr. John Wesley, 1703–1791.
15. (Old Tappan, N.J.: Fleming Revell Co., 1981).
16. Ibid.

Notes

17. Ross Foley, *You Can Win Over Weariness* (Glendale, Calif.: Regal Books, 1978), p. 128.

18. Ibid., pp. 131, 132.

19. See Raymond C. Ortlund, *Lord Make My Life a Miracle* (Glendale, Calif.: Regal Books, 1974).

20. Daniel H. Burnham, architect on the Chicago City Plan, quoted in *Air California*, May 1980, p. 69.

21. Andrew Murray, *The Two Covenants* (Old Tappan, N.J.: Fleming H. Revell Co., 1974), pp. 165, 166.

22. *Called to Maturity: God's Provision for Spiritual Growth* (Scottdale, Penn.: Mennonite Publishing House, 1960), pp. x ff.

23. See Anne Ortlund, *Up with Worship* (Glendale, Calif.: Regal Books, 1975).

24. Augsburger, *Called to Maturity*, p. 3.

25. "Turn Your Eyes upon Jesus," by Helen H. Lemmel, Copyright 1922. Renewal 1950 by H. H. Lemmel. Assigned to Singspiration, Inc. Used by permission.